Beer, Brats, and Baseball

Beer, Brats, and Baseball

ST. LOUIS GERMANS

JIM MERKEL

REEDY PRESS
St. Louis, Missouri

"By faith Abraham, when called to go to a place he would later receive as his inheritance, obeyed and went. . . ."
Hebrews 11:8

From Baden, Bavaria, and Saxony they came,

Five from a village of a hundred,

Fifty from a town of a thousand.

They were haters of injustice, misfits in their own land, unwilling to settle for the life of their fellows, anxious for a better world far away.

They changed their new land, and it changed them.

To all the Germans who enriched my home town,

To each of the huddled masses from every land who blessed our shores,

I dedicate the pages to come.

Reedy Press
PO Box 5131
St. Louis, MO 63139, USA

Library of Congress Control Number: 2012943930

ISBN: 978-1-935806-34-9

Photo credits:
  Concordia Historical Institute: 100
  Ed Golterman: 137
  Linda Gurney: 205
  Dorothy Johnson: 204
  Jim Merkel: 36, 66, 84, 88, 95, 116, 118-119, 125, 129, 138-139, 149, 179, 186-
  187, 189, 198
  Library of Congress: 2-3, 6, 36, 52, 154-155, 175
  Don Roussin: 159
  Schrader Funeral Home: 124
  SSND: 43, 78-79, 92

Please visit us at
stlouisgermans.com
facebook: Beer, Brats, and Baseball: St. Louis Germans
www.reedypress.com

Design by Jill Halpin

Printed in the United States of America
12 13 14 15 16   5 4 3 2 1

Contents

Preface

y great-great-grandfather must have been a hothead. What other name do you give a twenty-two-year-old who fights on the frontlines of a battle to gain liberty for his country? A freedom fighter? A radical? Either of those would work. Whatever the name, a family story has it that Louis Charles Merkel high-tailed it out of Germany in 1848 or 1849, worked at a piano factory in New York, and then brought his family to St. Louis in 1858.

Growing up, I often heard the story that my great-great-grandfather played a part in the Frankfurt Parliament, which made an ill-fated effort to write a constitution for Germany. "Upon its collapse, it was deemed advisable that he hurriedly leave," my father said. I can't prove it, but nothing I have found thus far makes it unlikely. Census records from 1860 show that my great-grandfather, Louis, was born in New York in 1857. His brother, William, was born in New York in 1855. The first record that Louis Charles Merkel and his family were in St. Louis was a notation in the 1859 St. Louis City Directory that showed he had started a piano factory at the residence of August Merkel near present-day South Broadway and Park Avenue. August and Louis likely were cousins or brothers.

Such facts thrill those seeking information about their ancestors. They thrilled me as well, but something was missing in the telling. How did they live? What went through their minds as they came to this city on the river? I have my own thoughts. A portrait shows Louis Charles Merkel with confident eyes and a close-lipped smile. His hair is fashionably cut, and he wears a goatee above an expensive, fashionable jacket. He must have been proud of the piano factory, especially after he moved it to the present site of Busch Stadium east parking garage. As an old radical, he must have made the short walk from there to the courthouse, where the slave Dred Scott began his court battle for freedom. That must have filled him with anger. That was the anger of the "Forty Eighters," who fought for freedom in Germany and then fought for the Union at the start of the Civil War. Historians agree the Germans played a key part in keeping Missouri in the Union. There is good evidence my great-great-grandfather was one of the Germans at Camp Jackson, the action on May 10, 1861, that ended any serious threat Missouri would end up in the Confederacy. Military records make it clear that he served in a military unit from September 1862 until he received a medical discharge in July 1863. He returned to his business, which was valued at thirty thousand dollars shortly before his death in 1885. As a comparison, in the same decade, author and publisher Mark Twain gave Ulysses Grant an advance of twenty-five thousand dollars to write his memoirs. Today, my brother, Louis Charles Merkel III, carries on the family business in its 154th year in St. Louis. I became a journalist and writer, offering proof that not everybody turned out right in this German family. Maybe this book will redeem me.

I would like to think my great-great-grandfather did something exceptional, but in truth, he was one of many German immigrants who came to St. Louis and did well. His story is just one more among the tales of thousands of Germans who came to St. Louis and the surrounding area starting in the 1830s. Their drive, and, yes, their German stubbornness, helped make St. Louis the place it is today.

Viel Spaß beim Lesen (Happy reading)

Introduction

Other composers in the same position might have stopped with eight symphonies. But as Ludwig van Beethoven's hearing loss became total, he persevered and composed one of the best musical works ever, his magnificent Ninth Symphony. What kept him going? A big reason may be his nationality. Beethoven was German, and Germans are not known for giving up. People who describe Germans use words like driven, compelled, determined, stubborn, and ordered to a fault. Some only half-jokingly use a psychological term: obsessive-compulsive. The description often is used in a negative sense, but it doesn't have to be. The word may size up how Germans might allow an idea, cause, or purpose to take them over, good or bad. The result was disastrous when Germans blindly followed Adolf Hitler down a path of destruction.

In the mid-nineteenth century, St. Louis contained thousands of Germans whose compulsions fell between the extremes of Beethoven and Hitler. One was Carl Wimar, an artist who toured the West. Wimar returned to St. Louis to paint vivid images of American Indians. Stricken with consumption, Wimar insisted on finishing a commission to paint murals of early St. Louis life on the inside of the dome of what is now the Old Courthouse in downtown St. Louis, even though it quickened his death. Adolphus Busch single-mindedly promoted the products of his father-in-law's brewery until their firm, Anheuser-Busch, was a leader in St. Louis and the nation. The radical St. Louis German newspaper editor Heinrich Boernstein wrote the fanatically anti-Catholic novel *The Mysteries of St. Louis*, ran a German theater, and helped stir up local Germans to defend the Union at the beginning of the Civil War.

Native Germans in 1861 were at the forefront of the fight for St. Louis. The Germans' instant willingness to fight for the Union traces to events in the Fatherland. Many had listened as parents and grandparents told stories of when Napoleon's armies changed the maps of Germany, Austria, and Russia in the first two decades of the nineteenth century. Napoleon's defeat at Waterloo freed Europe from his tyranny. But Germans remembered the political unity it brought in an otherwise divided land. At the start of the nineteenth century, Germany was merely a collection of small feudal kingdoms. In 1871 most of those states came together in the German Empire.

Poverty, famine, and what some saw as overpopulation also plagued the land of the Germans and gave them reason to leave. In the 1820s, a German lawyer and writer named Gottfried Duden came to Missouri looking for a place for fellow Germans to settle. His book about the land around the Missouri River led suffering Germans to believe a promised land awaited anyone bold enough to come. In 1848, Germany was caught up in liberal rebellions that swept through Europe. In Munich, the king of Bavaria turned power over to his son. Riots in Berlin caused King Frederick William IV of Prussia to call for an assembly to consider a German constitution. Soon afterwards, about six hundred delegates came together at a parliament in Frankfurt to discuss such a document. Hopes were high for a liberal and united Germany, but divisions within the Frankfurt Parliament brought efforts for permanent change to a halt. By early 1849, the liberal revolt was over and dictatorial governments were again in charge in Berlin and Vienna. Thousands reacted by boarding boats headed for America. Enough made their way to western cities like Milwaukee, Chicago, Cincinnati, and St. Louis for those towns to retain strong German influences today.

Many who came to St. Louis were still filled with the spirit of liberal rebellion that they believed was best exemplified by the American Revolutionary War. They hated slavery and anything that threatened the American Union. They already considered themselves freedom fighters. So it should surprise no one that thousands of St. Louis Germans signed up for volunteer units just a few days after Fort Sumter. When the Civil War ended, Germans settled down to brew beer, build new schools, and establish meeting places where people worshiped God in all kinds of ways or didn't worship God at all. They formed gymnastic associations called Turner Halls, established music associations, and relaxed in their beer gardens. Some entered politics and changed the look of St. Louis forever. Others started businesses. Immigrants held on to their language. Their kids spoke German at home but embraced the English they learned on the street or in school. Their grandkids never learned German.

Germans kept coming for the rest of the nineteenth century. The German-born population of St. Louis zoomed from 22,340 in 1850 to 50,510 in 1860. Native-born Germans made up about a quarter of the city's population but declined afterwards. Nonetheless, Germans in the nineteenth century were by far the biggest group of immigrants and much bigger than the other large group, the Irish.

Estimates are that more than 7 million Germans came to the United States from 1800 to the present, most between 1840 and 1914. Census figures showed the biggest ethnic group by national ancestry in 2000 was German. That year, 42.8 million Americans—15.2 percent of the whole—identified their ancestry as German. The 2010 census showed the biggest ethnic group was Hispanics, including Mexican, Puerto Ricans, Cubans, Spanish, and others Latinos. However, although the Census Bureau has yet to issue its 2010 ancestry report, it appears Germans will remain the largest single national ancestry group.

This Teutonic influence is particularly strong in Missouri, where 23.5 percent identified their ancestry as German in the 2000 Census. This is especially true in the Gateway City, where so many have German names. It's obvious in the names of our streets and schools, in our churches, and in our area's institutions. The story of what they did for the St. Louis area, especially in the last half of the nineteenth century, is remarkable.

Thankfully, many are discovering this history as they seek out their ancestors and make connections with sister city groups in Germany. They are celebrating their heritage by drinking German beer, learning the language, and listening to German music at Oktoberfests in St. Charles, Soulard, and at Jefferson County's Donau-Park. Americans want to know their heritage and how their ancestors contributed to society. This book reflects on the many amazing contributions of Germans to St. Louis and to all of America.

Beer, Brats, and Baseball

Rioting in St. Louis, 1861

Pioneers
before 1865

The Great German Victory at Camp Jackson

 orget the brewery. The greatest accomplishment of Germans in St. Louis was providing manpower for the Union takeover of a camp of Confederate-leaning Missouri state militiamen on the edge of town. The seizure of Camp Jackson, less than a month after Confederates took over Fort Sumter, ended any major threat that St. Louis, and with it Missouri, would fall into Confederate and anti-Union hands.

Ironically, a defeat in an earlier conflict made many of St. Louis's Germans willing to fight in this one. A number of the city's leading Germans at the start of the Civil War had fled their native land following failed efforts to make change in their country in 1848. They were sensitive to injustice and looked askance at slavery. Many had been soldiers in Germany and so were capable of a new fight. Radicalized by the likes of Heinrich Boernstein, the rabble-rousing editor of the St. Louis German newspaper *Anzeiger des Westens,* they were ready to provide the backbone to keep Missouri in the Union. Besides this, Germans had the muscle to act. More than one out of four St. Louisans in 1860 were born in Germany.

The city's Germans rejoiced when Abraham Lincoln won the presidency in 1860. Then they watched as states moved toward secession. They also viewed with dismay the actions of Missouri's newly elected governor, Claiborne Jackson, who leaned toward secession. They offered help to Congressman Frank Blair Jr., a leader of the Union cause in Missouri. Jackson eyed the federal arsenal at St. Louis and persuaded the state legislature to transfer power over the St. Louis Police Department from the city's mayor to a police board appointed by the governor. Days after Confederates began the bombardment of Fort Sumter on April 12, 1861, President Lincoln asked for 75,000 volunteers. Jackson refused Lincoln's request for 3,123 volunteers from Missouri.

He called it illegal, unconstitutional, and revolutionary.

In response, Blair arranged for the German members of his Home Guard to be sworn in as Missouri Volunteers. Jackson then summoned the eastern portion of the Missouri Militia to an annual encampment near present-day Olive Street and Grand Boulevard in St. Louis. He planned to use siege guns provided by Confederate President Jefferson Davis to bombard the arsenal near present-day Broadway and Arsenal Street. Captain Nathaniel Lyon, the arsenal's commander, refused the police board's demand to vacate the premises. On the sly, he shipped everything in the arsenal that wasn't immediately needed to Illinois.

As America moved toward war, more than ten thousand St. Louisans signed up for three-month stints under Lyon. Eighty percent of those volunteers were German. Put into perspective, nearly one out of six of the more than fifty thousand German inhabitants of St. Louis enlisted. On April 21, word came that secessionists had seized the federal arsenal at Liberty, Missouri. By May 10, Lyon was convinced of the danger Camp Jackson posed. That day, he took advantage of the newly fattened army at St. Louis by marching six thousand to eight thousand men to the camp and demanding its immediate surrender. His position hopeless, camp commander General Daniel Frost surrendered the seven hundred to nearly one thousand men at the camp. It was a peaceful surrender.

As soldiers returned with prisoners, a riot ensued. Civilian bystanders threw rocks and brickbats and heckled, "Damn the Dutch." A drunken man tried to push through the Union ranks, was pushed back, and then fired a shot, wounding an officer. Shots killed one man and wounded Captain Constantine Blandowski, a Polish patriot born in Prussia. Volunteers shot into the crowd, fatally wounding fourteen to twenty-eight bystanders, depending on the source. The number of injured was placed at forty to as many as one hundred. "This sad final act cast a dark veil over an otherwise glorious day," said the St. Louis German paper, *Westliche Post*. But the Union had won a victory, and Germans bore the credit. Soon, Union soldiers took over the state capital at Jefferson City, completing what amounted to a

German Victory at Camp Jackson

Union-sanctioned coup against the legal state government. Jackson fled to southwest Missouri.

After the war, General Ulysses S. Grant—who witnessed the events at Camp Jackson—wrote that a Confederate takeover of St. Louis would have made a major difference in the war. "It would have been a fearsome task to reconquer St. Louis, one of the most difficult any commander could have. Instead of a campaign before Vicksburg, there would have to be a campaign before St. Louis." Fifty years after Camp Jackson, Wilhelm Kaufmann considered acts of German Americans in the War Between the States in his book *The Germans in the American Civil War*. Concerning the events of May 10, 1861, he wrote, "This provided the Germans with the occasion for a great independent deed, their most glorious single deed throughout the entire Civil War." Descendents of Germans who made that victory possible can take pride in their ancestors' accomplishments.

The First of Many

Twelve years after it was founded, the little village of St. Louis was a mishmash of Frenchmen, Creoles, Spaniards, Indians, and black slaves. As of yet, Germans had little reason to come, because they didn't have colonies in the New World. But German priests doing mission work had every reason to come, for they sought not land nor gold, but souls.

In 1776, a priest was the first German to arrive in St. Louis. Father Bernard de Limpach had lived on the Rhine and likely was born in Limpach, a town in Luxemburg. A member of the Capuchin branch of the Franciscan Order, he came to St. Louis from the German Coast, an area along the Mississippi generally between present-day New Orleans and Baton Rouge where Germans had settled.

Priests had been in the village since its founding in 1764, but Father Bernard was the first pastor of a St. Louis parish. He was there because of an edict from King Charles III of Spain, which ruled Louisiana at the time. The king sent the Capuchins to Louisiana, and the Capuchins sent Father Bernard to St. Louis. Far from his home, he presided for thirteen years over the spiritual needs of the village during a formative time of its history.

Father Bernard blessed a new church and set about building a two-story stone rectory. "Father Bernard was much beloved by his congregation, and traditions are still preserved of his piety and zeal," wrote J. Thomas Scharf in his book *History of St. Louis City and County*. Humdrum church records made of Father Bernard's service note that from the time he arrived in May 1776 to his departure in November 1789, he baptized 410 whites, 106 blacks, and 92 Indians. He officiated at the marriages of 115 whites, one black, two Indians, and one mixed white and Indian, while performing the funerals for 222 whites, 60 blacks, and 44 Indians. In addition to St. Louis, he also cared for souls in Carondelet, St. Charles, present-day Florissant, and Portage de Sioux.

Besides the usual comings and goings, the records note that on April

17, 1780, he blessed the first stone of a fort for the town. Named Fort San Carlos, for Charles III, king of Spain, the fort went up after the American revolutionary George Rogers Clark warned the Spanish commander of St. Louis that the British planned to make mischief in the village. On May 26, 1780, Indians, fur traders, and troops commanded by the British attacked St. Louis. Protected by the fort, cannon fire, and two hundred defenders, the villagers fought back the attack. But about twenty-one were killed and seventy captured. Father Bernard recorded that he buried that day in the parish cemetery "the bodies of Charles Bizet, Amable Guion, Calve and son and a negro Chancelier massacred by the Indians."

St. Louis never again came under attack, and Father Bernard went about his business as before. But something was stirring in the priest. He wanted to return to the German Coast. In 1787, he wrote a letter to his superiors asking for a reassignment to that area. "The parish, which is very numerous, has four villages depending on it, and these increase daily by the emigration of French families here, to be free from the vexations of the Americans who are on the eastern side of the river," he wrote. "If I insist on a removal, I am guided by the hope of finding somewhere else an alleviation to my bodily and to mental trouble. Everything else is of no consideration to me."

In the autumn of 1789, he received a new assignment, as pastor of St. Gabriel, Iberville, in present-day Louisiana. He arrived there in February 1790. The next year, he became pastor in nearby Pointe Coupee, which he served until he died in 1796.

Father Bernard de Limpach

The first German to arrive in St. Louis

How Gottfried Duden Sold Missouri

ottfried Duden didn't fit the normal picture of a farmer who works from dusk to dawn milking cows, feeding chickens, and plowing fields. Before breakfast, he hunted for partridges, doves, squirrels, and turkeys. After breakfast, this gentleman farmer read his books and strolled his garden until lunch. When the midday meal was finished, he rode his horse to visit his neighbors or to enjoy the beauty of the 270 acres he owned in present-day Warren County, Missouri. He got to know his neighbor, Nathan Boone, son of Daniel Boone. He hired others to do the actual farm work.

Duden didn't intend his farm to be a true source of income or livelihood. Instead, he was a travel writer, scouting land for Germans he hoped would come. His gushing reports back to Germany were responsible for much of the flood of German immigrants who came to Missouri and St. Louis from 1830 through the 1850s. An attorney, Duden came to America in the mid-1820s to find the best area where Germans could immigrate. He had become convinced that Germany was hopelessly overpopulated and saw opportunity in the empty lands of the western part of the United States. So he came to St. Louis in 1824 with Ludwig Eversmann, who was the son of a mine surveyor in Berlin. From there, they explored both sides of the Missouri River before settling on the land he bought in Warren County. He spent the next three years taking notes on the people, farming, animals, and other aspects of life along the Missouri River. He brought those notes back to Germany in 1827 and published his findings in the 1829 book *Report on a Journey to the Western States of North America*.

Much of the book contains specific descriptions of the land and how an immigrant could survive. But scattered throughout are words of praise for this Rhineland of the New World likely more so than proper.

More than twenty years before Indiana newspaper writer John Soule first penned the words, "Go West, young man," and longer still before Horace Greeley popularized that phrase, Duden was saying similar things to his countrymen. "People in Europe will not and cannot believe how easy and how pleasant it can be to live in this country. It sounds

Bericht

über eine Reise

nach den

westlichen Staaten Nordamerika's

und einen mehrjährigen Aufenthalt am Missouri (in den Jahren 1824, 25, 26 und 1827), in Bezug auf Auswanderung und Uebervölkerung,

oder:

Das Leben

im

Innern der Vereinigten Staaten

und dessen Bedeutung für die häusliche und politische Lage der Europäer, dargestellt

a) in einer Sammlung von Briefen,

b) in einer besonderen Abhandlung über den politischen Zustand der nordamerikanischen Freistaaten, und

c) in einem rathgebenden Nachtrage für auswandernde deutsche Ackerwirthe und Diejenigen, welche auf Handelsunternehmungen denken,

von

Gottfried Duden.

Gedruckt zu Elberfeld im Jahre 1829 bei Sam. Lucas, auf Kosten des Verfassers.

Title page to Duden's Report

too strange, too fabulous," he wrote. "Believing in similar places on this earth has long been consigned to the fairy-tale world. The inhabitants of the Mississippi area, on the other hand consider the reports of need in Europe exaggerated."

The cynic might call such words crass salesmanship, akin to the pitchman extolling the benefits of Florida marshland, but Duden was sold on Missouri himself, and comments peppered through the book show it. Besides, poverty was great in Germany. The land was a collection of small city-states, and most people had few options. "Because of its clear skies, the state of Missouri is far more conducive to health than Germany," he wrote at one point. "Anyone who manages his farm with some degree of skill enjoys an abundance of the best food. No one worries about a roof over his head or protection against the cold of winter. He also made a prediction that came true: beer brewers would soon become rich along the Mississippi, because it then was brought from elsewhere. Lansing Hecker, today's honorary German consul for the St. Louis area, acknowledges Duden was writing as a romanticist. "It sounded pretty good to people who were having difficulty in terms of famine and war." With the low prices of the land, "They could buy a quarter section, six hundred acres, and they could be a real landowner."

Duden's words won over many. His *Report* helped lead to the creation of numerous societies encouraging Germans to move to Missouri, and his book was at the top of the list of reasons why Germans began flooding into Missouri and St. Louis starting in the early 1830s. Some immigrants were disillusioned and said they didn't find what Duden promised. One critic, Gustave Koerner, toured the Missouri River from St. Louis to Jefferson City and found many Germans who came there after reading Duden's report. Many were bitter that Missouri wasn't the place Duden promised, Koerner said. "I deem his 'Reports' of the region of the country of which he speaks and of the conditions the emigrants are expected to find there, as too flattering and too vividly colored," he wrote. Duden's American Rhineland may not have been Eden. But for those who persisted, there were riches in Missouri they'd never known in Germany.

A Rabble-rouser
to the End

here are no better words to describe Heinrich Boernstein than the cliché "larger than life." He edited the biggest and best German newspaper in St. Louis, was the main force behind the city's German theater, and prepared his community for the Civil War. He led a regiment at the beginning of the war in an action that kept St. Louis on the Union side. But for all of this, Boernstein possessed characteristics that made him less than admirable. He wrote a German-language novel that was outrageously anti-Catholic, and he was an unrepentant rabble-rouser.

The story of how Boernstein got to be that way began in Hamburg, Germany, where he was born in 1805. In 1813, his parents moved to Austrian-controlled Poland, where he grew up writing and acting. After a stint in the Austrian Army, he studied medicine at the University of Vienna before becoming a journalist. In Vienna, he wrote plays and was secretary of two theaters. The 1840s found him in Paris, where he was named manager of that city's German Opera. As editor of a German-language cultural publication in Paris, he briefly worked with Karl Marx, who later wrote *The Communist Manifesto.* Boernstein was an ardent supporter of the 1848 revolt that led to the dethroning of King Louis-Philippe, but he left for the United States after the rebellion went astray.

Boernstein worked as a doctor in Highland, Illinois, before he was asked to edit the German-language newspaper *Anzeiger des Westens* in 1850. He carried the Democratic Party banner, since all but a handful of Germans were Democrats. He battled Know Nothings and Nativists. But his newspaper's anti-Catholicism made possible an unspoken alliance between German radicals and Nativists to make life miserable for the Irish. Boernstein's influence became so great that papers favoring the Whig Party screamed he was trying to Germanize St. Louis.

To boost his paper's readership, he wrote the German-language potboiler *The Mysteries of St. Louis; Or, the Jesuits on the Prairie des Noyers, A Western Tale* and serialized it in the *Anzeiger des Westens*. It includes murder, burials alive, a sprinkling of sex, and themes that condemn Catholicism, especially the Jesuits. Steven Rowan, an editor of a modern edition of the novel, speculates that a midnight meeting on Bloody Island in the book could have provided inspiration for a scene in the wildly anti-Jewish polemic *The Protocols of the Elders of Zion.* All of those elements offered by a normally powerful writer weren't enough to make *The Mysteries of St. Louis* a good read. "Hastily written, it is spectacularly bad," wrote one reviewer, Frederick C. Luebke of the University of Nebraska–Lincoln.

Boernstein also founded an anti-Christian "Society of Free Men," in which members took delight in skewering Catholics and Lutherans alike. In another endeavor, he leased the St. Louis Opera House and presided over the performance of such works as *Faust, Romeo and Juliet,* and *William Tell.* One of the first things the city police did after the Confederate-leaning state government took them over was to shut

Heinrich Boernstein

Theater, Journalism, Politics

down Boernstein's opera. And, being a German, he ran a beer hall in his printing plant and set up a brewery.

His greatest task, though, was his fight to prevent St. Louis from falling into Confederate hands. He helped warm St. Louis Germans to the new Republican Party and Abraham Lincoln. When the arsenal at St. Louis was in danger, he was among German newspaper editors who printed appeals for volunteers. He commanded a German regiment that took over Camp Jackson, the state militia encampment that threatened the arsenal. Soon, the old Austrian Army soldier was military commander of the state capital of Jefferson City.

His future seemed unlimited in America, but then President Lincoln appointed him U.S. consul in Bremen, Germany, in August 1861. He left for Germany, only to return to St. Louis once more the next year to fight for gradual emancipation of slaves against radicals demanding immediate abolition. Heavily denounced in this country, Boernstein returned to Bremen. His son, who had been put in charge of the *Anzeiger des Westens*, shut it down in 1863 and joined the Union Army as a major commanding a new African-American battalion. The *Anzeiger* reappeared as a Democratic paper and remained alive in various forms until 1912.

Relieved of duty in 1866, Heinrich Boernstein never returned to America but moved to Vienna, where he became a theater director and wrote dispatches to American German-language papers. He and his wife, Marie, died in 1892 and were buried in Vienna. Their tombstone declared they had died Americans. In 1941, Nazis destroyed their grave. Even in death, Boernstein was stirring things up.

The Scholar Farmers

I n 1832, nearly five hundred members of the Giessen Emigration Society came to Missouri to start a German settlement. Disgusted by the barbarity of slavery, roughly thirty-two of the new immigrants left the group and crossed into St. Clair County, Illinois, and settled. A flood of their countrymen followed in the decades to come, and the German influx greatly influenced the development of the Illinois county.

The group that came in 1832 chose to live as farmers in the Shiloh Valley and soon were known as "Latin Farmers." The words weren't always used in praise. American farmers said the Germans were able to talk to each other in Latin but couldn't plow straight. To that settlement came many immigrants who escaped Germany after a rebellion in Frankfurt was put down in 1833. Among them were George Engelmann, a botanist who worked with Missouri Botanical Garden founder Henry Shaw, and Gustave Koerner, a politician and confidante of Abraham Lincoln. With the first settlers, these later Latin Farmers saw agriculture as superior to life in town. "The student, the scholar, the doctor of philosophy, the professor, the merchant, all wanted to become farmers," noted the author of the 1881 book *History of St. Clair County, Illinois, with Illustrations Descriptive of its Scenery and Biographical Sketches of Some of its Prominent Men and Pioneers*. "A few succeeded, while others returned to their former occupations or to public life."

If farming wasn't their forte, they still saw success. They and other German immigrants founded newspapers, businesses, distilleries, factories, and civic groups and were at the center of the area's political life. The group included the first mayor of Belleville. Theodor Krafft was thirty-seven when he was elected Belleville's first mayor in 1850, the year the town was incorporated. He held numerous political positions and was president of one of Belleville's most important institutions— the Belleville Philharmonic Society Symphony Orchestra. Founded in 1866, the group plays the music of the masters to this day.

It's no surprise that Germans accomplished so much in St. Clair County. In 1850, 57.1 percent of adult males in St. Clair County were born in another country. Of those, 78.5 percent were Germans. When the Civil War came, they were united in fighting for the Union. And unlike some in the first group, later Germans made skilled farmers. One observer noted at the time that many German farmers who had arrived poor ten years before now owned one hundred acres or more. After they came, they would hire themselves and their children out. Then the children would help them build a cabin and start a farm with a yoke of oxen and a cow. Their first harvests fed them while they used money earned when they hired themselves out to buy farm equipment. They may not have known Latin, but they did know how to plow straight.

Of Vagabonds, Secessionists, and Workers' Lunches

he games Louis Kessler played were the least of his problems. "It is no crime to be a gambler, but it can be shown that Kessler has worked professionally *at cheating at cards* for several years, and has suffered for it occasionally, though not as much as he has deserved," Friedrich Muench railed in the *Mississippi Blaetter* on August 2, 1858. Besides that, Kessler had been dishonorably discharged from a volunteer company during the Mexican-American War. But the *Blaetter*, the Sunday edition of the St. Louis German-language newspaper *Westliche Post*, had more against Kessler, a German candidate for St. Louis County jailer. "K. is a slaveowner, a slave trader, and a slave breeder, not due to education or inheritance but because the business is profitable, comfortable, and pleasing for him," Muench wrote. The paper relished the scoop because its German-language rival, *Anzeiger des Westens*, had endorsed Kessler. The *Anzeiger* backed off that endorsement when Kessler's past became known.

Such vitriol was as typical in German-language newspapers in St. Louis of the mid-1800s as it was in English-language newspapers of the same period. Whatever their language, editors loved to expose hooligans, vagabonds, and ne'er do wells, especially politicians. Steven Rowan, a professor of history at the University of Missouri–St. Louis, caught the flavor of the German-language press in *Germans for a Free Missouri: Translations from the St. Louis Radical Press, 1857-1862*. Many translations, such as the one about Kessler, dealt with politics and events leading to the Civil War, but others reported the comings and goings of the city's German immigrants.

An ad in the *Mississippi Blaetter* on May 17, 1858, invited one and all to the Spring Festival fundraiser for the Deutsches Institut in Concordia

Park the following weekend. On April 3, 1859, the *Mississippi Blaetter* pondered how the city's workers of all strata ate together. "At lunch all differences of rank are abolished and socialistic equality reigns supreme; the fancy luncher, who sees the lunch as a luxury or an occasion for entertainment, stands shoulder to shoulder with the poor devil who fate has treated unkindly and whose rumbling tummy would soon sing elegies or even dirges if lunch did not still that longing which has no name," the paper said.

However, tales of the nation's lurch toward Civil War filled much of the pages of the city's antislavery German-language press. On March 8, 1858, the *Mississippi Blaetter* editorialized against a proposal to reintroduce the slave trade, as long as slaves were freed after fifteen years. "You buy a grown rascal of thirty years of age and throw him to the devil when he is forty-five and getting stiff—what could be more advantageous?" On October 23, 1859, the *Blaetter* noted a report by the English-language *Missouri Republican* that a group of immigrants that had just arrived from Germany included a black man who wore the same clothing as the others, spoke German, and smoked a German pipe. "We can only hope he brought good papers with him so some trader in human beings does not seize him as 'fleeing goods' and sell him South," the paper said.

The German-language newspapers thoroughly reported on the lead-up and outbreak of war. They noted Abraham Lincoln's election as president and how Germans fought to stop Missouri's secession. "The North has awakened from its slumber; the earth shakes under the tread of its legions, and the South trembles," the *Westliche Post* declared on May 1, 1861. "So let us get to it and clean this Augean stable so that freedom can prosper in purer air." Like so much writing in nineteenth-century newspapers, it was not objective reporting, but the writing was as good as anything in English, and it prepared its readers for war.

When Tragedy Became Farce

he first play performed in German in St. Louis was meant to be a tragedy, but it was closer to theater of the absurd. As St. Louis German newspaper editor Heinrich Boernstein related the tale in his memoirs, the performance started when a down-on-his-luck actor named Herr Riese showed up in town in 1842. Seeing the dire need of the man from Berlin, some fellow German immigrants offered to help him ply his trade. They rented a room above a German tavern called *Zum Bremer Schlüssel* and prepared to produce Friedrich Schiller's tragedy *The Robbers*.

As with all pioneers, producers had to improvise. They couldn't find an actress to play the character Amalie. So players talked about her, but she never made an appearance. That was the plan, anyway. Then there was the matter of the armchair where a character called the Old Moor was to sit. The group lacked such a chair, but somebody found a crate and covered it with a bed sheet. What happened next was either by accident or mischievous intent; no one is sure. Somehow the bed sheet became tangled with the curtain. When it went up, the bed sheet rose with it, and the Old Moor fell on his *boden*. The audience roared.

More trouble ensued when the performance resumed. Hunting rifles and revolvers used for the robbery scene made sufficient noise, but they also filled the place with thick gun smoke that wouldn't go away. Then Riese refused to perform the fifth act unless he could stab an Amalie as the script demanded. So the tavernkeeper's cook volunteered, or was volunteered, to assume the role. Riese brought the knife down, but when she didn't collapse just so, he slugged her.

Few people saw anything else; the smoke was too thick. People coughed too much. No matter. At the end, the audience still cheered.

Then—good Germans all—the actors went downstairs to the tavern and drank away their profits. People liked *The Robbers* so much that the company put it on again in Belleville. Once again, the actors celebrated afterwards by investing all their profits at a tavern. A brewer hauled the stranded pack of pickled performers back to St. Louis in his wagon. The company was no more, but a tradition of German theater was born in St. Louis.

The Man Who Made the Garden Great

n its seventy-nine acres, the Missouri Botanical Garden contains more than four thousand trees, the largest traditional Japanese Garden in the United States, a tropical rainforest in its Climatron conservatory, and a bushy Victorian-style maze. Visitors to the Garden at 4344 Shaw Boulevard in South St. Louis spend hours sampling its delights without coming close to discovering all it has to offer.

Even if those visitors did see everything at the Garden, they may not know about one of the most significant parts of its work. The Research Division has nearly fifty doctoral-level botanists and maintains or participates in projects in more than thirty countries. The Garden maintains a herbarium with well over six million dried plant specimens, some hundreds of years old. Garden archivist Andrew Colligan explains that a herbarium can be thought of as a library of dried plants for study and reference. All of that important work had its start with the German-born physician and botanist Dr. George Engelmann. "We consider him the godfather of the Research Division at the Garden here," Colligan said. Without Engelmann's influence, the Garden likely would have been only a display garden, he said. By doing so, Engelmann took what would have been a good public garden and made it a great one.

As with so many early Germans, Engelmann came to America primarily because of the turmoil and lack of opportunity in Europe. Born in 1809 in Frankfurt-on-the-Main, he began his lifelong work in botany while still a teenager. He showed his interest in botany in the dissertation he wrote for his degree of Doctor of Medicine in 1831. As published in 1832, his study of large plants included detailed illustrations by Engelmann. His future might have been bright in his native land, if it hadn't been for political upheaval. Agents of the government spied on students and professors and quashed efforts at intellectual freedom.

Engelmann was forced to transfer from the University of Heidelberg to the University of Berlin after he participated in a short and failed student protest. Frustrated with the lack of movement toward German unification and intellectual freedom, he also was discouraged by hard times in his own country. Then an uncle said he would pay Engelmann's way to America if he would invest money for him in the new land. That was enough to bring him to the United States.

Engelmann arrived in Baltimore in December 1832 and made his way to St. Louis. Soon, he was joined by an uncle, Frederick T. Engelmann, and his family. Together, they established a farm near Belleville, Illinois, where George Engelmann started his scientific experiments. He stuffed wild birds, recorded daily temperatures, worked with snakeskins, and started collecting plant specimens.

After establishing a medical practice in St. Louis, Engelmann widened his interest and collected samples in Arkansas and the Indian

George Engelmann

Botanist, Shaw's Garden

Territory. He became an expert on cacti, conifers, and grapes. As his reputation grew, he helped form the St. Louis Academy of Science, which later was a primary force in the creation of the Saint Louis Science Center. And, in the late 1850s, he met retired hardware mogul Henry Shaw, who had made up his mind to establish a premier botanical garden modeled after the ones he had visited in Europe. Asa Gray, a preeminent naturalist at Harvard University, and Sir William Jackson Hooker, the director of the Royal Gardens at Kew, both encouraged Shaw to go beyond the mere display of plants and make his garden a center of research. Shaw was surprised to learn that the man they recommended to start this work, Engelmann, lived in St. Louis.

Fortunately for Shaw, Engelmann was already planning a trip to Europe. He sailed with his family in November 1856 and brought back books, plant specimens, and information on cacti. By the time Engelmann died in 1884, the collection he helped establish was so large that it overwhelmed the museum building at the garden. More space became available after Shaw died in 1889. As Shaw's will stipulated, his townhouse at Seventh and Locust streets downtown was dismantled and moved to the Garden. The plant specimens and books he collected were moved to the townhouse. Today, that collection remains a vital part of the Garden's library and herbarium. The work Engelmann did was priceless, and he apparently didn't put a price on it. He wasn't an employee or what today would be called a consultant. Engelmann was never paid for his work for the Garden. He did it for the benefit of science.

A Wasted Act
of Heroism

he tale of Carl Ferdinand Wimar's death is so noble that any story of his life should start there. In 1861, the artist received a prestigious commission: painting murals on the inside of the dome of the courthouse in downtown St. Louis. But Wimar, who was known for his paintings of American Indians, was sick with consumption, a disease that may or may not have been tuberculosis. He took the commission anyway and set about painting the dome, even though it sped his demise. As he weakened, he was carried up the stairs to his scaffold. One night he came home spent and told his wife, "This is my last work; when the dome is finished I shall be finished with me." He died when the dome murals were completed, on November 28, 1862, at the age of thirty-four.

It's probable that Wimar's half-brother August Becker painted the dome from instructions and drawings Wimar gave him. But that doesn't diminish the heroism of Wimar's last act or the brilliance of the artwork.

Wimar, whose actual first name was Charles, was born near Bonn, Germany, in 1828. His father died, and his mother remarried Matthias Becker when he was seven. Becker came to St. Louis by himself in 1839 and sent for his family in 1843. In Germany, Wimar had familiarized himself with the Indians in James Fenimore Cooper's books. In America, his poor understanding of English made it hard to make friends, but he grew close to Indians who lived nearby. They told him their stories, and one taught him to use the bow and arrow.

Wanting to find a trade for their son, the Beckers helped him obtain a position with Leon de Pomarede, a painter specializing in frescos. Around 1849, de Pomarede took Wimar to the Falls of St. Anthony in Minnesota. Their task was to find material to paint the stretch of the Mississippi River from the place it became navigable to the Ohio River.

The Lost Trail
by Carl Wimar

During his time with de Pomarede, Wimar started making paintings that are still on display today.

When Wimar was younger, a sick traveler came to his home. As the family nursed him back to health, Wimar told him of his dreams to be an artist. The man strengthened and left. Now word came that he had died and left Wimar money he needed to go overseas to study. Legal fights prevented Wimar from getting the money. But hope that the money would come provided him with the encouragement he needed to travel to Duesseldorf, Germany, around 1852.

After returning in 1856, Wimar traveled west in 1858 and 1859 to make sketches for his paintings of American Indians. His paintings and drawings often showed muscular Indians in buckskin coats and headdresses, frequently with a yellow sun setting behind them. Many show them hunting buffalo on horsebacks.

Wimar was now widely known for his paintings of the American Indian, and some said Wimar himself looked like an Indian. He received commissions from the highest level of St. Louis's society. He was so prolific that he produced forty-five paintings from the time he returned to America until his death, a period of six years. But his health was failing, and his success didn't translate into financial security. He took on other projects to bring in more money.

One project was painting figures on the dome of the St. Louis Courthouse—now the Old Courthouse—with his half-brother August Becker. He offered to do the work for five hundred dollars. Those who offered him the project raised the price to one thousand dollars. Sick with the disease that would kill him, he worked on eight figures. The top four represented law, liberty, justice, and commerce. Below, on four concave "lunettes," were scenes of De Soto's discovery of the Mississippi River in 1541, the city's founding in 1764, the 1780 attack by British and Indians on St. Louis, and Cochetopa Pass in the Rocky Mountains.

In spite of his failing health, he finished the project and died. Almost immediately, the work started to fall apart. Bad chemistry in the plaster, dirt buildup, and incompetent restorers ruined almost everything. In 1881, an artist painted over the top four pictures. Later, restorers made it worse. More recent work brought out some of Wimar's design. Still, the muddy images on the lunettes are nothing like the crisp, bright vistas in his other works. Wimar's gesture of spending his last days creating a masterpiece at the Old Courthouse truly was heroic. In hindsight, though, it probably wasn't the best idea.

A Big Mouth Fights for Liberty

osef Hecker could have offered the remark in disgust, but he said it with fondness when he told his son Friedrich, "Where ever did you get that big mouth?" From the beginning, Friedrich Karl Franz Hecker spoke out for the ideas of individual liberty embodied in the American republic, so much so that he led a rebellion to establish them in his native Germany in 1848. A lifelong hothead, he fled to America when that quixotic revolt failed. But the principles he championed are today recognized in the German Constitution. In America, he established a farm near St. Louis, worked closely with Abraham Lincoln to form the Republican Party, and led two regiments in the Civil War. Children in Germany today learn about him in school, but in America, he is largely ignored. In Germany, the ideas he espoused may have been revolutionary, but they were typical in America.

Friedrich was born in 1811 in Baden, the son of the royal court councilor. Once, his father wrote a letter to the Grand Duke of Baden attacking a new income tax system that seemed to tax peasants unfairly, even as it reduced the privileges of the nobility. As he grew into adulthood, Friedrich become a lawyer and studied American principles of the likes of Thomas Paine.

Then came 1848, when democratic revolts swept through Europe. Friedrich Hecker wrote the list of human rights included in the Offenburg Resolution of March 1848. That list was included in the post–World War II German Constitution. On April 12, he and the Socialist Gustav Struve issued a call for a general uprising in Baden. Eight days later, a large force of Hessian and Baden troops defeated the little band that rallied behind them. He fled to Switzerland and then to America, where he was received warmly in New York and other German population centers. Although he returned briefly to Germany in 1849, he spent the rest of his life in America.

From then on, home was a farm in Summerfield, Illinois, about twenty-eight miles east of St. Louis. In the daytime, he worked the farm, grew grapes, and made wine. At night, as he had been in Germany, he was an advocate for radical republicanism, but with an American bent. He corresponded frequently with Abraham Lincoln and German-Americans and promoted the new Republican Party. He was fifty when the Civil War started, but that didn't stop him from coming to St. Louis to sign up as a private with Colonel Franz Sigel's 3rd Missouri Volunteer Regiment. Perhaps to get rid of someone he thought was too old to fight, Sigel told him to go back to Illinois and organize troops there.

Hecker soon was offered command of the 24th Regiment, Illinois Volunteers, also called the Hecker Rifles Regiment. The unit of German volunteers from the Belleville, Illinois, area soon collapsed because officers weren't confident in Hecker's ability to lead. Then he was offered a new command of the 82nd Illinois Volunteers. He did better in this command but was injured in the Battle of Chancellorsville. A snuff box deflected the bullet and prevented worse injury. He recovered but found himself in trouble in an action in the Battle of Wahatchie in Tennessee in October 1863. Major General Joseph Hooker accused him of being lax in responding to a call to come to the aid of Brigadier General John Geary during the battle. A court of inquiry backed Hecker, but he'd had enough. Passed over for promotion to brigadier general, he resigned early in 1864.

Hecker spent the postwar years at his farm, writing and fighting for the Republican Party. He was applauded by some during a return trip to Germany in 1873, but criticized by others who said his speeches were outdated and reflected the views of a revolutionary twenty-five years behind the times in Germany. Even after he died in 1881, his words caused consternation. He wrote in his will that he wanted his heart cut out and buried in Germany, but by the time the will was read, his body was already in the ground. Figuratively, his heart may have stayed in Germany, but his family refused to dig him up and send his real heart there. For once, practical concerns won out for this most impractical man.

Lincoln's German Friend

hen the Republican Party's national convention opened in Chicago in May 1860, many said Abraham Lincoln didn't have much of a shot to be its nominee. Gustave Koerner disagreed. As much as anyone, the German immigrant politician from Belleville, Illinois, made Lincoln's nomination possible. So close was Koerner to Lincoln that he was the only pallbearer at the president's burial who was not from Springfield, Illinois.

Born in Frankfurt-on-the-Main, Germany, in 1809, Koerner studied at the universities of Munich and Heidelberg, and received his law degree in 1832. He took up arms in a revolt in Frankfurt on April 3, 1833. The French government sent him to Switzerland, but he sneaked back to Paris. From there, he made his way to Le Havre, France, and sailed for New York. In 1833, he arrived near Belleville and established a farm. He became convinced the work of German travel writer Gottfried Duden promoting Missouri as a place for Germans was inaccurate. Duden's observations led many in Germany to come to Missouri. Koerner presented what he thought was a more balanced view in his own writings.

On Christmas 1833, he continued a German tradition. Not able to find fir trees in that area, Koerner relied on a Christmas tree a friend made for him from the top of a sassafras tree. It was festooned with apples, candles, colored pieces of paper, ribbons, and nuts. "Perhaps this was the first Christmas tree that was ever lighted on the banks of the Mississippi," Koerner wrote in his memoirs. But the law, not tree decorations, was Koerner's passion. After studying law at Transylvania University in Lexington, Kentucky, he was admitted to the Illinois Bar in 1835. Ten years later, he was appointed to the Illinois State Supreme Court. In that position, he first became acquainted with Lincoln the lawyer. Illinois voters elected Koerner lieutenant governor in 1852. Soon he was caught up in the rising crossfire over slavery. In 1856, he left the Democratic Party and campaigned for the Republican presidential nominee, John C. Fremont. Along with Abraham Lincoln and others, he became a leader of the Republican Party. He was president of the state Republican convention in 1858 that nominated Lincoln for U.S. senator from Illinois and set the stage for the Lincoln-Douglas debates.

In 1860, Koerner was at the center of efforts to nominate Lincoln for president. Lincoln was a dark horse, but he had one advantage: the Republican convention was in Chicago. Later, Koerner wrote: "I am pretty certain that, had the convention been held any other place, Lincoln would not have been nominated." Koerner packed the convention center with cheering Lincoln supporters. He also arranged to get a place on the platform committee and pushed through a plank guaranteeing foreign citizens' rights. While most Germans didn't support Lincoln before his nomination, Koerner persuaded them to get on his bandwagon afterwards. His job at the convention finished, Koerner joined a delegation on a train to Springfield to tell Lincoln he had the nomination.

Koerner turned to campaigning for Lincoln. He gave speeches, organized campaign groups, and wrote articles. After the election, he pressed Lincoln not to yield to pressure to let the South secede in peace. "If we could not live together in peace as one nation, we certainly could not live together in peace as two nations," he advised. "Even Civil War was preferable to the destruction to our Union."

When war came, Koerner organized a German volunteer unit, the 43rd Illinois Regiment. Lincoln then assigned him to the staff of General John C. Fremont. He was among the German leaders who ensured people of his nationality backed the Union. In 1862, Lincoln appointed him U.S. Minister to Spain. There, he persuaded Spain to stay neutral during the Civil War and eased its concern that the United States would move against Spain in Cuba. He came home in 1864, campaigned for Lincoln's re-election, and resumed his law practice.

Koerner was walking to work in Belleville on April 15, 1865, when he saw flags at half-mast and heard the news of the death of his friend. "Lincoln's death was everywhere considered a national calamity. The rebels had lost their best friend, was the general expression," he wrote. He became disillusioned with corruption in the Republican Party and made a failed run for Illinois governor for the new Liberal Republican Party in 1872. He died in 1896, after telling his story in a two-volume memoir. He made his influence known during a revolt in Germany in the 1830s and on the state of Illinois, but his greatest accomplishment was helping to get Abraham Lincoln elected president. Of Lincoln, Koerner wrote, "He was the justest man I ever knew."

Much More Than
a Journalist

arl Schurz is one of three people honored on "The Naked Truth," a monument to great St. Louis German journalists. But had the statue in St. Louis's Compton Hill Reservoir Park noted great St. Louis German-American politicians, speakers, soldiers, or public servants, he would have been just as deserving of having his name on it.

Like many Germans who came to St. Louis, Schurz was in the midst of the revolt in his country in 1848. Born near Cologne, Germany, in 1829, he was studying history, philosophy, and ancient languages at the University of Bonn when revolution broke out. That ended his study and began an adventure for the books. "The voice of the professor sounded like a monotonous drone coming from afar," he wrote later. "We closed our notebooks with a sigh and went away, impelled by a feeling that now we had something more important to do—to devote ourselves to the affairs of the Fatherland." Schurz joined with University of Bonn Professor Gottfried Kinkel in calling for rebellion in Bonn. When that failed, Schurz fled to Rastatt, Germany, where he was captured. He escaped by hiding for three days in a sewer and making his way to Switzerland. Kinkel also was captured and locked in the fortress of Spandau. Schurz returned to Germany, rescued Kinkel and came to Paris, where he wrote for German papers. He moved to London, married the daughter of a Hamburg merchant, learned English, and crossed the Atlantic to start life in Wisconsin.

In America, politics called. Backing the new Republican Party, Schurz made unsuccessful efforts to run for governor and lieutenant governor of Wisconsin. Debates between Stephen Douglas and Abraham Lincoln were subjects of his first English speech. That well-publicized address helped lead to a series of speeches throughout the country on the coming conflict. As a Civil War general, he was in the thick of it, serving at the Second Battle of Bull Run, Fredericksburg, Chancellorsville, and Gettysburg. After the war, he edited a newspaper in Detroit and bought part of the St. Louis German-language newspaper, the *Westliche Post,* in 1867. Then he came to St. Louis, where he became the paper's editor.

Some criticized such papers for separating Germans from others and keeping them from learning English. He defended the papers. "That the existence of the German press tells for the preservation in this country of the German language as a language of social and business intercourse is to a limited extent true. But what harm is that?" One of his greatest accomplishments was the hiring of Hungarian Joseph

Carl Schurz

editor of the *Westlich Post*

Pulitzer, who would go on to found the *St. Louis Post-Dispatch*. Pulitzer, Schurz, and another *Westliche Post* editor, Dr. Emil Preetorius, were members of a chess club that met in the St. Louis library.

In 1869, politics called again, and the Missouri Legislature named Schurz a U.S. senator. After leading a revolt against President Ulysses Grant, he retired from the Senate and resumed his work at the *Westliche Post*.

Life took Schurz elsewhere after he accepted President Rutherford Hayes's appointment as Secretary of the Interior in 1877. After he left that post in 1881, he was named managing editor of the *New York Evening Post*, contributed to *Harper's Weekly*, and died in New York City in 1906. That was two years after he returned to St. Louis to speak at German Day at the St. Louis World's Fair and called for close relations between the United States and Germany. After a long career in his adopted land, Schurz had distinguished himself in far more ways than the creators of "The Naked Truth" noted.

The One They Fought "Mit"

alf a century after the Civil War, young Americans would sign up to fight following the call "Uncle Sam wants you," but in St. Louis at the start of the War Between the States, the words that stirred Germans to enlist with the Union were "I goes to fight mit Sigel." Gehrhard *und* Berthold, Conrad *und* Dietrich all heard the words and stepped forward to battle against Confederates, both at Camp Jackson and in later encounters for the Union—no matter that Franz Sigel muffed it as a general. Until the end, Germans thought too much of him for the Union to send him away.

Like many German leaders in St. Louis at the start of the Civil War, Sigel built his reputation during the German Revolution of 1848–49. Born in 1824 in the Grand Dutchy of Baden, he trained at the Karlruhe Academy and joined the army of Baden's Grand Duke. When the revolution began, he resigned and placed his lot with the revolutionaries. He commanded an army of the Liberals and was named minister of war of a provisional government in 1849.

When Prussians crushed the rebellion, he fled to Switzerland and then to France. There he met the communist theorist Friedrich Engels and Carl Schurz, who would go on to be a Civil War general and a St. Louis newspaper editor after the Civil War. Worried he could face arrest in France, Sigel fled to England, where he met such radicals as Karl Marx, author of *The Communist Manifesto.*

When he arrived in New York in 1852, Sigel was met as a hero. He married Elsie Dulon, whom he had met in England, and came to St. Louis to teach at the Deutsches Institut in 1857. He plunged into the fight against slavery and worked for the new Republican Party. He also wrote for papers, including the radical Republican *Westliche Post,* and was named a district superintendent in the St. Louis Public School System. As America moved toward civil war, he spoke against secession. Then, as a German-American known for his military experience in 1848, he signed up to help defend St. Louis's arsenal. Though he was actually a colonel, Germans started calling him "general" and joined him in arms.

Sigel commanded the 3rd U.S. Volunteers under Captain Nathaniel Lyon during the Camp Jackson Affair on May 10, 1861. But Sigel only was in charge of his unit for a short time. North of the arsenal, Sigel's

Franz Sigel

German Civil War commander

horse slipped on the pavement and fell, injuring Sigel's leg. He rode in a carriage later to the camp.

Sigel continued to fight and was present when Lyon, now a general, was killed on August 10, 1861, in the Battle of Wilson Creek in southwest Missouri. Sigel led the 2nd Missouri Brigade in a brave but failed flanking operation at the battle. He was named a brigadier general and played a role in the effort to drive Confederates from Missouri. After that, Sigel showed mixed results and became a target of criticism. Many of the critics said he showed the arrogance typical of a German intellectual and had a Prussian military technique that didn't fit in America.

Sigel commanded a division at the Battle of Pea Ridge near Bentonville, Arkansas, on March 7–8, 1862. While Sigel's supporters credited him with the victory, others said it wasn't deserved. At the Battle of Cedar Mountain in Culpeper County, Virginia, on August 9, 1862, Sigel was criticized for being late to help the Union center after Thomas "Stonewall" Jackson attacked Union forces.

Some heaped blame on Sigel for his role in the Union defeat at the Second Battle of Bull Run. The criticism continued, but President Abraham Lincoln kept supporting Sigel because of his German following. Lincoln's patience ran out following a major defeat at New Market, Virginia, on May 15, 1864, when Confederate General Jubal A. Early outflanked him and almost made it to Washington, D.C. Sigel was relieved of his command on July 8, 1864, and resigned on May 4, 1865. After the war, Sigel became a newspaper editor and switched to the Democratic Party when Samuel Tilden ran as a reform candidate in the 1876 presidential election. Sigel was appointed U.S. Pension Agent for New York by President Grover Cleveland, and died in 1902. His shortcomings as a military leader were obvious, but he fought with passion for liberty, in Germany and in America.

Das Deutsche Haus

Middle Years
1865–1945

There are Names . . .
and There Are
German Names

ow blessed were St. Louis Germans Henry Noll and Otto Rung? With a nationality known for double "m's," double "n's," double vowels, and "sch's" in multi-syllable last names, the monikers of Noll and Rung were simple and hard to misspell. It was useful for them when they signed up for the overwhelmingly German Missouri Volunteers at the beginning of the Civil War. Pity the poor person who had to write the more difficult German names by hand on lists of those who also volunteered: Hy Zudderrovest, Captain William A. Hequembourg, Mich. Feuchtenbemer, Herman Strattelgahan, and Nic. Schwartztrouble.

Eventually, peace came, and the city's Germans went about making their livings and their names. Unfortunately, some still had names they might have wanted to unmake. One of them, Dietriche Sommerfruechte, owned a popular tavern on Broadway. Around Pine and Main was the F.W. Aufderheide Commission House. An actress with a difficult name, Fanny Janauscheck, performed in St. Louis during a visit here from Germany. The dry goods store Buddecke & Droege was on Fourth Street near Convent Street, along with Brandtstetter's bakery, John Wamsganz's shoe store, and Biedenstein's grocery.

There was purpose behind those names, or at least originally. The name of Julius Weinbrecht, chairman of the academic committee of the Concordia Turners, meant "wine breaker." Perhaps an ancestor stomped on grapes for a living. Two words emerge from a translation of the last name Henry Koenigkraemer, another of the Germans in the Missouri

Volunteers. "Koenig" is "king" or "ruler," while "kraemer" means "grocer," "shopkeeper," or "owner" of a small retail store. Joseph Spiegelhalter's last name meant "mirror holder." It was nothing like his actual profession of physician and city coroner.

The more difficult German names may have been descriptive in Germany and a source of pride in America. But here they also made life harder for those who had to spell them. The answer for many German Americans anxious to fit into their new homeland was to shorten and Americanize their names. The "vons" in the names were dropped. "Geltmann" became "Goldman." They often eliminated a syllable in a four-syllable name. Today the task of spelling many German names is not as hard as it once was. But it's still too easy to render "Schroeder" as "Shroder."

Feuchtenberner
Schwartztrouble
Zudderrovest

Why Schools Stopped Teaching German

In the mid-nineteenth century, German was the chosen tongue around Main and Second streets. In that area near the riverfront, merchants and craftsmen reveled in speaking the language of the Fatherland with German customers. "There was a time that one who passed through this street could imagine himself transplanted to Germany, for one heard only German spoken here," St. Louis German journalist Ernst D. Kargau wrote in his 1893 book *The German Element in St. Louis.*

German wasn't quite as prevalent in other parts of the city before the Civil War, but it was still there. There was a reason it was impossible to escape the sound of the German tongue. In 1850, 29 percent of St. Louis's inhabitants started their lives in Germany. The percentage dropped to twenty-six when census-takers made their rounds ten years later, but it was still enough for Germans to save the day for the Union at Camp Jackson. And the more than 50,000 Germans, out of 190,000 city residents, was enough for them to ensure their language would still be heard on the streets of St. Louis.

In 1837, a year before the first public school opened, the school board denied requests by Germans to include their language in its curriculum. The state only lets us teach English, the board explained. So Germans established their own schools. By 1860, the 5,524 students in the city's German private and parochial schools were nearly as many as the 6,233 students in public schools. Buckling under German pressure, the school board introduced German in five schools in 1864. The experiment proved a success. By the 1887–88 school year, more than 21,000 students were taking German and English.

But bilingual education couldn't go on forever. In 1870, the census showed the first-generation German population had grown nearly 9,000 in ten years, to more than 59,000, but the city's population was growing

German-language education

even faster. As a result, first-generation Germans made up only about 19 percent of the city's population in 1870, 15 percent in 1890, and 4 percent in 1920. With that decrease came a decline in German influence. Attacks on German-language education were inevitable.

The first assault was in the name of budget austerity. An 1879 school board election pitted those who would eliminate German-language education against those who would keep it. The *Globe-Democrat* opined that Germans learn their language at home and not at school. Dropping it would save $60,000, the paper said. But the *Post-Dispatch* noted a third of the children who studied the language weren't of German descent. Possibly influenced by Joseph Pulitzer, its German-speaking Hungarian co-publisher, the paper wondered whether opponents had other motives. "This subject should be considered with candor and without prejudice. Especially should there be no appeal to the prejudices of birth or race," the paper said. German-language education in public schools survived, but only temporarily.

In November 1887, each side faced off in another election. The *Missouri Republican* argued German and English couldn't be taught thoroughly together in primary grades. The German *Anzeiger des Westens* complained the *Republican* was being nativist. On election day, opponents of German-language education easily won, even in heavily German areas. Even Germans didn't care that much. The new school board laid off ninety-four German teachers and stopped German instruction.

German teachers were allowed to keep teaching the language in public schools after school. Some German groups tried to teach the language on their own. In 1909, the school board allowed it on Saturday mornings in schools in German areas of the city. When the National German American Alliance held its annual convention in St. Louis in 1913, Alliance President Charles Hexamer made an obligatory appeal for German-language education, but bilingual education never was popular. World War I snuffed it out. In truth, it had been dying for years. It was the victim not of anti-German sentiment, a drop in influence, or budget cuts but of German assimilation into American society.

The Music of Their Souls

I n 1837, a new German resident of St. Louis watched in disgust the funeral march of a member of the Odd Fellows. A trio, armed with a bass drum, a clarinet, and a violin, rattled the dead with a less-than-glorious rendition of *"Adeste Fideles."* "I thought if there are only a few musicians in St. Louis, I will soon change that," he later wrote in his autobiography. Two years later, he performed at a more proper Odd Fellows burial, complete with two funeral marches he had composed and a double quartet of male voices and two chorales.

The musician was William Robyn. Born in southern Holland, near Prussia, in 1814, he quit school at twelve to study piano. A year later, he was playing at balls. By sixteen, he was teaching piano. Professor Bolte, a friend of Mozart, Beethoven, and Haydn, taught him flute and clarinet. It was no surprise, then, that a wealthy man hired him in 1836 to teach his children how to play the harp, guitar, flute, and horns. The man sought to bring his family to the German community of Hermann, Missouri, the next year. He thought his children could entertain themselves on those instruments. Alas, sweet music blossomed into love between Robyn and one of the man's daughters, Catharine Wurz. The man opposed the union, but Robyn persevered. The father finally agreed, but only if Robyn came to America. The couple married in February 1837 and traveled to the new land. On the way west, Catharine's first child was born in Cincinnati. They continued on a boat to St. Louis. But Catharine couldn't travel further, so they remained.

Early on in St. Louis, Robyn witnessed the butchering of a Christmas song and started teaching and playing music. In one event, he played waltzes in breaks between a man demonstrating the ways of laughing gas and some Indians who sang and performed war dances. Soon he organized the first music society in St. Louis, called the "Philharmonic." Its fare ranged from such pieces as "Home Sweet Home" to a French operetta. He also founded a group called the St. Louis Brass Band.

Around this time, another early orchestra started playing at Concert Hall in St. Louis. Then in 1845, William Robyn became musical director of the St. Louis Polyhymnia Society. Its first concert, on October 8, 1845, included Gioacchino Rossini's overture to *La Gazza Ladra* and Mozart's "Overture to Don Juan." Its monthly concerts were purely instrumental, since no amateur women singers could be persuaded to sing with the orchestra. That may have been the reason the society shut down in 1855.

Others kept trying. A new organization showed itself in 1860: the St. Louis Philharmonic Society. The next year, the group hired a German conductor and composer named Eduard de Sobolewski as musical director. Sobolewski, who hailed from Koenigsberg, East Prussia, conducted such pieces as "He Watching Over Israel" from *Elijah* by Beethoven and the works of composers like Mendelssohn and Rossini at the first concert of the first season in 1860 at Mercantile Library Hall. Sobolewski left for Chicago after six years, and by 1870, a lack of money forced the Philharmonic to cease operations.

In 1871, violinist and conductor Robert Sauter organized the Haydn Orchestra, a group that played throughout the 1870s. Then in 1872, the national Triennial Saengerbundfest (singing society) came to St. Louis. Germans organized other groups, including the Jaegar Saengerbund, Saengerbund of the Sons of Hermann, and the Liederkranz Singing Society.

The time was right in 1880 for a permanent organization to perform the works of the masters. That year, a German organist named Joseph Otten, just twenty-eight, organized the St. Louis Choral Society. The next year, he added an orchestra to accompany his singers. The group he founded became the world-renowned Saint Louis Symphony Orchestra. German conductors such as Alfred Ernst and Max Zach continued the influence of the Fatherland on the orchestra and the city. An examination of old symphony programs shows that many of the orchestra's members had German names.

A Noble Scam

Adolph von Donkberg may have claimed he was a German count, but a certain Miss Beckman sized him up as a no-account. He showed up in St. Louis in December 1882 with a letter of introduction from a Professor Wieder of Berlin to his brother-in-law, a Mr. Boeckeier, a local lumber merchant. He was slender, well-dressed, with hair parted in the middle and a slight mustache. He never said at the start of a conversation that he was a nobleman, but the subject always came up. Soon he was the toast of St. Louis German society, including a Mr. Ledergerber, who was collecting money for victims of floods in Germany. Donkberg volunteered to help at Ledergerber's office, where he encountered Miss Beckman. She smelled a *ratte*. Donkberg enthusiastically opened the mail but was told to leave after a few days. Fourteen dollars of collections money was noted as missing.

Meanwhile, von Donkberg was running up a tab at a downtown hotel. Any day, he told the patient folks at the hotel, money would come from Germany so he could pay his bill. In time, they'd had enough and tossed him out. He found lodging with a German woman downtown, but he didn't pay her either. Then he told a benefactor he had a chance to find work with a surveying party, but he needed to borrow a theodolite, a precision instrument used in surveying. The benefactor got him in touch with the president of Saint Louis University, who loaned him one. He promptly pawned it for five dollars and vanished.

Police tracked him to Chicago, where he'd actually found work—real work—as a porter. He was arrested for the theft of the theodolite and brought back to a St. Louis jail. There, he told a *St. Louis Post-Dispatch* reporter his real name was Graf von der Dannenberg. He produced a letter from a lawyer in Germany claiming he had 200,000 marks in the Fatherland. All of twenty-three, he claimed his woes began when he was a second lieutenant in the Ninth Hanoverian Dragoons, stationed in Metz, Germany. The lawyer was appointed to watch his affairs after he went deeply into debt. He was dismissed from his military post after he fatally wounded an opponent in a duel. Then he came to America. The lawyer once sent him $150 through a German consul, but it was sent back after he didn't pick it up in time. In jail, he harbored hope that his money finally would come and he could pay his way out of jail.

A Leg Up

I n the Olympic Games, six medals—three gold, two silver, and one bronze—would be a stunning achievement for the most accomplished athlete, much less a competitor with a wooden prosthesis for a left leg. George Eyser earned these honors not in the paralympics for the disabled mind you, but in the 1904 Olympic Games in St. Louis.

Eyser, who was born in 1871 in Kiel, Schleleswig-Holstein, Germany, competed in gymnastics events as a member of a team from the Concordia Turnverein in St. Louis. He gained his medals in gymnastics events that didn't require the use of a leg, but he wasn't shy about competing in events he had no chance of winning. He came in dead last in the one hundred yard dash, the long jump, and the shot put of the twelve-event All-Around competition. He finished tenth in the other nine events and seventy-first overall in the All-Around.

Eyser came to the United States at the age of fourteen and first lived in Denver. He moved to St. Louis and made his living as a bookkeeper for a construction company. Before he lost his leg in a train accident, he didn't show much of an interest in exercise. But afterwards, the South Side resident did all of the workouts he would find at the Concordia Turners, located just around the corner from Adolphus Busch's brewery and not too far from Eyser's home at 2851 South Jefferson Avenue. Like all Turner groups, the Concordia Turners focused on a program developed in Germany to build strong bodies and strong minds. It worked with Eyser.

In the 1904 Olympics, Eyser took gold in the Horse Vault, the Parallel Bars, and Rope Climbing. In the Horse Vault, he had to jump over a long horse without using a springboard. He won silver in the Side Horse and the four-event Men's Individual All-Around, while he won bronze in the Horizontal Bar. He moved with style. "When running and jumping, he wears an artificial leg, with which he makes prodigious leaps across the ground," said a 1908 article in the *St. Louis Post-Dispatch*. "When exercising on the horizontal bar or the 'horse,' he either removes the cork leg or straps it closely to the sound leg."

The article appeared on May 24, 1908, as Eyser prepared to go with a team from the Concordia Turners to an international tournament in Frankfurt-on-the-Main, Germany, that July. The final rehearsal before the event was a public exhibition at the Concordia Hall. Then it was off to Germany to compete with fifty thousand athletes from all over the world under the eye of Kaiser Wilhelm. When it was over, the team emerged victorious, as it did when it won the National Turnfest in Cincinnati in 1909.

Ironically, the record of that team and of its superstar with an artificial leg isn't well known at the Concordia Turners today. And it wasn't highly praised during the 1904 Olympics in St. Louis. Papers that were full of items about the World's Fair hardly wrote about the Olympics. The international competition had not yet captured the world's imagination and attention.

Eyser's victories were among the highest points of one of the worst years in modern Olympics competition. It didn't help that the Olympics seemed to be just another act of the Louisiana Purchase Exposition. Slightly more than 100 of the 681 participating athletes were from outside the country, mainly from Canada. The man first given the gold medal in the marathon was an American who made most of the trip in a car after he couldn't keep running because of cramps. Eyser helped bring redemption to the games in a year they needed it.

The next time a person with an artificial leg went to the Olympics was in 2008, when swimmer Natalie du Toit from South Africa competed in the South African marathon. Du Toit, who had lost her left leg in a traffic accident, wound up in sixteenth place. Eyser did much better in a time when people were less forgiving of the physically challenged. His triumph was one of the greatest in Olympic history.

Hope at the Fair

In thirteen years, Americans would know German Kaiser Wilhelm as a monster among rulers. They would call his German subjects Huns or any other awful name people at war give to their enemies. Americans of German heritage would have to show again and again their loyalty to the United States. But that seemed unthinkable on October 6, 1904, German Day at the St. Louis World's Fair. "The German-Americans will have possession of St. Louis today," the *St. Louis Globe-Democrat* editorialized. The *St. Louis Republic* newspaper guessed it was the second-largest event at the fair up to then after St. Louis Day.

Actually, Germans and Germany made their presence known at the fair from the start. Germany's national pavilion, "Das Deutsche Haus," featured a reproduction of the breathtaking Charlottenburg Castle near Berlin. The Constabulary military band from the Philippines welcomed the arrival of Prince and Princess Hohenlohe-Schillingfuerst on May 5, 1904, the day the fair formally opened, with paint not yet dry. The Palace of Varied Industries included a Monumental German Hall, with forty-eight rooms, complete with furniture, German toys, and numerous other items. Built for $750,000, the Tyrolean Alps was among the most expensive attractions. Local German-America restaurateur Tony Faust was president of a concession in the Tyrolean Alps that served as many as twenty thousand in a day. Shrimp, crab, game, poultry, frogs, and other delicacies kept the fairgoers' tummies full and their faces smiling. In one day, fifty cooks, sixty assistants, and five hundred waiters went through twenty-five to thirty heads of cattle, twelve hogs, twelve sheep, twelve lambs, half a ton of poultry, six hundred to a thousand loaves of bread, and seventy-five pounds of coffee.

As fabulous as those attractions were, they were only preparation for German Day. On that day, more than two thousand children performed calisthenic drills. Members of local German-American Turner organizations paraded, people cried when a band played "*Die Wacht am Rhein*," and German and American patriotism seized the day. "May this day be

celebrated in undisturbed pleasure as a worthy testimonial of what, in the astonishing development of the great trans-Atlantic republic, the German immigration signifies," the Kaiser wrote in a cablegram to those at the event.

It was a day for speeches, congratulations, and hope for peaceful relations between the two nations. The speakers included Carl Schurz, a German immigrant, Civil War general, and former presidential cabinet member who worked at St. Louis's German-language newspaper the *Westliche Post* and was a U.S. senator from Missouri in the late 1860s and early 1870s. "We German-Americans are the hyphen between Germany and America; we present the living demonstration of the fact that a large population may be transplanted from one (country) to another country and they may be devoted to the new fatherland and yet preserve a revered love for the old," Schurz said. Emil Preetorius, a longtime German-American journalist for the *Westliche Post*, honed in on the same points in his speech. "Truly, to be good Americans, we need not become indifferent Germans," Preetorius told the crowd. "On the contrary, the best Germans are also the best Americans." It was a worthy sentiment, offered at a place designed to make people hopeful for a better future. Had sense prevailed, more people would have considered those noble thoughts in the rush to start the First World War.

The Family Business
That Changed Chemistry

oung Edward Mallinckrodt reached for a book in his father's bookshelves and found one by the German chemist Justus von Liebig. He kept reading and developed a lifelong interest in carbon, oxygen, hydrogen, nitrogen, and so much more. His German-immigrant father did what he could to see that young Edward would grow to produce the stuff that could cure disease and go into products not yet invented. He put a laboratory for his son in a brick outbuilding on his farm. Edward and his brothers Otto and Gustav went on to found a company that pioneered numerous chemicals for medical care and one very important one in World War II. For nearly a century Edward and his son Edward Jr. led that firm, Mallinckrodt Chemical Works.

Edward's father was Emile Mallinckrodt, who bought land for a farm along the Mississippi River in present-day North St. Louis after he came here from Prussia. As the brothers prepared to start a chemical company, Gustav learned the business end working for a drug company. Edward and Otto studied the craft in Germany. When Edward and Otto returned in 1867, the three brothers founded G. Mallinckrodt and Company. The first plant—three wooden sheds and a stone acid house—was on the family farm. To provide the money for the project, Emile borrowed $10,000 on the farm.

The company was the first west of Philadelphia to make chemicals for medicine and other processes requiring high levels of purity. As Mallinckrodt met the needs of the western part of the nation, it prospered. In time, Otto and Gustav died, and Edward ran the company himself. Under him, plants started in such places as San Francisco, Denver, Detroit, and Philadelphia. Among the wealthiest men in St. Louis, Edward was quick to help other North St. Louis industries. A biographer, James Cox, wrote that he is "a St. Louis man in every sense of the word, and he is one of those citizens who never tire in their efforts to advance the city's interests and to uphold its good name whenever and wherever it may happen to be assailed."

By the twentieth century, Mallinckrodt produced more than five hundred chemicals. Around that time, Edward was joined by his Harvard-educated son Edward Jr. Born in 1878, he distinguished himself at Mallinckrodt by making improvements in ether that made it a safer and more comfortable anesthetic. He succeeded his father when he died in 1928. Edward Sr. willed $2 million to a fund to be distributed to various charities by his son. People estimated he gave the then-huge amount of $1.5 million to charity during his lifetime.

The company grew until it received a major assignment in World War II. While scientists had purified small amounts of uranium in labs, they couldn't produce what was needed to make a chain reaction and then an atomic bomb. Within three months after Mallinckrodt started, it made a ton a day of high-quality uranium oxide. The product was used in the first successful chain reaction at the University of Chicago in 1942. For several years, Mallinckrodt was the nation's only maker of pure uranium.

After the war, Mallinckrodt made chemicals for jets, fluorescent and television tubes, synthetic rubber, and plastics. The junior Mallinckrodt gave away much of the money he made. In awarding him its annual Humanities Award in 1962, the *St. Louis Globe-Democrat* noted he supported a lengthy list of charities, from Washington University Medical School to Saint Louis University to Harvard. The *Globe* took note that in 1931, before Social Security, Edward Jr. started a generous retirement program for his workers. At eighty-four, the balding, mustachioed senior statesman was driven to work every day at the plant on the site of the old family farm. "Mr. Mallinckrodt is friendly and considerate toward his employees," the paper noted. "He knows many of them personally, particularly the older ones."

It was a last hurrah for Edward Jr. and a family run company. He retired as board chairman in 1965 and died in 1967, a century after his father and uncles founded the company. Seven years later, Mallinckrodt, Inc. announced it was considering moving its headquarters to the East Coast after it couldn't get a zoning change needed to move to a site in west St. Louis County. Instead, it moved to a different tract in the county—so ended the company's stay at the family farm. In 2000, Mallinckrodt agreed to be bought by Tyco International (now Covidien). The health-care conglomerate continues the name in its product line, but it has little of the character of the original German owners.

A Terrible Time
to Be German

In 1845, John Kaiser decided to go into the wholesale grocery business. For three quarters of a century, the business thrived. George E. Kaiser and William Huhn later took the enterprise over and named it after themselves. But then the United States entered World War I, and people took second looks at the Cass Avenue company's delivery wagons. The name Kaiser-Huhn Grocery Co. seemed unpatriotic when American soldiers were fighting the Kaiser and Germans were called Huns. Hecklers would shout "Kaiser Hun" and sometimes pelt the company's delivery wagons with rocks. So the company changed its name to Pioneer Grocery.

Unlike the Japanese-Americans during World War II, German-Americans during World War I generally weren't forced into internment camps. But in the hysteria of the First World War, people with German names were forced to demonstrate their loyalties and ignore their heritage. Those who didn't comply might be forced to kiss the American flag, as one hundred men in Staunton, Illinois, had to do. At least they weren't tarred and feathered, as two people were in the same incident. "No official complaint of a disturbance has been made," Staunton Police Chief Benjamin Vollentine said. "The only report I have received is that there are a lot more Americans in Staunton today than there were yesterday." In Collinsville, Illinois, a German alien was hanged by a mob that heard he had denounced the United States and President Woodrow Wilson. High school students no longer could take German as a foreign language. Libraries pulled German-language books from shelves. Berlin Avenue in the Central West End was renamed Pershing Avenue, so any victory parade of returning soldiers wouldn't be on a street with such an unpatriotic name.

Enemy aliens—citizens of countries like Germany—were prohibited from going into restricted zones without permission. The zones included downtown St. Louis and bridges across the river. William H. Busch was one enemy alien who ran afoul of the law. A German citizen, he was visiting the United States when the war started and couldn't return. After Busch applied for a permit to go into restricted zones, the proprietor of the rooming house where he was staying came forward. She said that when Busch told her he was going to move, she reminded him he had to let the police know of his plans. To that, he supposedly said, "To hell with the police and to hell with America. The first chance I get, I am going back to Germany and help them lick everybody." For that, he was arrested on an order that he be interned for the rest of the war.

German-Americans who uttered words that might be taken as disloyal faced jail time under the Espionage Act. One who had to defend himself against prosecution was Dr. Charles H. Weinsberg, who was president of the State Alliance of the German-American National Alliance until it was disbanded. After he told reporters that the German and Austrian forces would win, he was put on trial for disloyalty. A federal judge dismissed the charges after Weinsberg's attorney said that he was uttering his personal opinion without disloyal intent and that he didn't know the comments would be published. In truth, the American press fought for the rights of the Germans. The German-American papers worked to show that German-Americans were loyal Americans like everybody else. Many German-Americans fought and died in the war. But it didn't remove the stain left when Americans were persecuted only for having the same blood as their enemies.

The Tragic Death of Robert Paul Prager

eople said things were getting ugly for anyone who didn't toe the patriotic line in the spring of 1918. It was especially so for those of the same nationality as our German enemies in World War I. In some cases, people were beaten, tarred and feathered, and run out of town. But no one was as much a victim of this wartime hysteria as Robert Paul Prager.

A socialist, Prager emigrated from Germany to America in 1905. Nonetheless, he offered plenty of evidence he was as patriotic an American as anyone and that he was fully in favor of the war against the Kaiser. He had a man arrested and jailed for thirty-two days for protesting Prager's display of an American flag. Two American flags were found in his room. But Prager had a flaw: his temper. A baker, he decided to advance himself by becoming a miner. But his application to join the miners' union was rejected, possibly because he was an active socialist. The union's president called him a liar and a spy. In response, Prager handed out flyers disputing those claims and declaring his allegiance to the union and the nation. He claimed the president wanted to send a mob against him and have him arrested.

But others said he attempted to convert miners to socialism and had spoken negatively about President Woodrow Wilson and the United States. That was enough for a group of miners to seize him on April 4, 1918, and force him to kiss the American flag. He escaped to the boarding house where he lived. A group of miners then went to his home and made him walk barefoot on the streets of Collinsville with an American flag on his back. Fearful for Prager's life, Collinsville police took him and put him in jail for his own safety. Mayor J. H. Siegel begged the mob to leave Prager alone. "We do not want a stigma marking Collinsville," he admonished the crowd, "And I implore you to go to your homes and discontinue this demonstration."

The mob disbanded, but only for a while. Then three hundred people, some cheering, others waving flags, stormed the jail and dragged the terrified Prager away. When the self-styled patriots stopped at the tree where they intended to hang Prager, they asked him if he had anything to say. "Yes," he said. "I would like to pray." He wrote a letter to his parents, Mr. and Mrs. Carl Henry Prager, in Preston, Germany. "Dear Parents," it said. "I must this day, the 5th of April, 1918, die. Please pray for me, my dear parents. This is my last letter. Your dear son, ROBERT PAUL PRAGER." Then Prager knelt down, placed his hands on his breast, and implored God for three minutes.

Shortly after midnight, Prager was hanged on a tree west of Collinsville. And the world was quick to react. The act made headlines from St. Louis to Germany, where the German press condemned the lynching.

On May 13, eleven Collinsville residents went on trial in the case. In his closing argument, State's Attorney J. P. Streuber said, "The man who justifies mob rule is a disloyalist. Any man who says America stands for mob rule is a traitor." But defense attorney Thomas Williamson said, "The war situation has developed a new 'unwritten law.'" That law allowed people to murder to protect themselves from disloyalists, he said. In his instructions to the jury, Judge Louis N. Bernreuter said jurors should disregard any such law and only consider whether Prager was lynched. The jury deliberated forty-five minutes before declaring the defendants not guilty. Because it was dark the night of the lynching, the jury said, it was uncertain who did the crime. Today, Prager is buried at St. Matthews Cemetery at Bates Street and Gravois Avenue in South St. Louis. On his tombstone are the words, "the victim of a mob."

Stuff for the Movies

t was a perfect plot for a John Ford Western. Told of some troublesome sermons by the pastor in a tiny town, a group of agitators promised to come get him. Hearing this, the pastor alerted his parishioners, who stationed two townspeople with guns at each of the four roads leading into town. Two more watched from the church's bell tower, ready to ring the bell if they saw the men, so people from outside the village would come to help. Barbed wire stretched across the bridge at the south end of town. At night, children and mothers watched uneasily as the man of the house picked up his shotgun and prepared to stand guard. The sheriff, meanwhile, let the group know that if they came, they would go home in "wooden overcoats." They never came.

It's gripping stuff, and it really happened, but not in the Wild West. It took place in the German-American hamlet of Maeystown, Illinois, thirty-five miles south of downtown St. Louis. The pastor was Paul Schulz of St. John Evangelical Church. As recounted by local historian Gloria Bundy in two books on the history of Maeystown, Schulz's offense was preaching in German during World War I. While the groups of "patriots" who made the threats never came into Maeystown, they terrorized other communities nearby, Bundy noted. A German minister in another community was not so lucky. He was tied to a tree and made to believe he would be burned at the stake. He never recovered from the trauma of the event.

Bundy also related a story about a Maeystown resident late in the 1800s who had enough with the taunts of non-German "Yankees" who lived nearby. After spending several hours drinking in Maeystown, the Yanks would harass village residents. One day, a villager got so tired of the abuse that he went home to get his gun, came back, and shot one of the Yankees. Then he hid in the attic of Christian Muether, a local shoemaker. The minister in Maeystown could have told the avenging villager to turn himself in. Instead, he advised him to leave town as soon as possible. The man and his family moved to St. Louis. So it was that a sad chapter of American history played itself out in a small corner of Illinois.

A German standoff

Dr. Max Fights the Flu

n enemy was coming to St. Louis, and Dr. Max C. Starkloff was the general charged to stop it. The deadly invader was a worldwide influenza pandemic that would kill more than two-thirds of a million people in the United States and 30–50 million people worldwide in 1918–19. In St. Louis, the bug killed 1,703 people and infected 31,500, but it would have been far worse if it hadn't been for Starkloff. The German-American city health commissioner used emergency powers granted by the city charter to close schools, churches, theaters, movie houses, and a bevy of other places where people could come together and spread the menacing disease. He forced streetcars to ride with windows open.

Businessmen opposed the policies as Draconian, but Starkloff had the support of Mayor Henry W. Kiel, who had defeated Starkloff for nomination for mayor in 1913. So for six weeks in October and November 1918, churches stayed empty on Sunday, movie houses were dark at night, and St. Louis's death rate from the epidemic was far less than cities like New York, Philadelphia, Pittsburgh, Boston, and Cleveland.

Starkloff seemed made for the days when he would shut down St. Louis and save hundreds of lives. His father was Dr. Hugo Maximilian (Max) von Starkloff, a son of a German baron. After Dr. Hugo came to America in the early 1850s, he married Hermine Auguste Reinhardt. Max C.—a shortened version of Maximilian Carl—was born in 1858, the third of the Starkloff children. Max would not be the only member of his family who would do notable things. Hugo Maximilian was U.S. consul to Bremen, Germany. Max's half-sister Irma S. Rombauer wrote the original much-loved cookbook *The Joy of Cooking*. Rombauer was the daughter of Hugo Maximilian von Starkloff and Emma Kuhlmann von Starkloff, who married Hugo after Hermine Starkloff died. Max

Starkloff, the grandson of Max C. Starkloff, became a quadriplegic in a car crash in 1959 and spent the rest of his life as a much-honored advocate for the disabled.

With that heritage in his future and past, Dr. Max C. Starkloff's achievements are less surprising. After his 1881 graduation from St. Louis Medical College, he worked as a doctor on the South Side and as chief surgeon at the Vulcan Iron Works. In ten years at the Iron Works, he treated four injuries a day, or fifteen thousand for the decade. These days, a factory with that kind of record would get a visit from OSHA. Back then, doctors just kept busy patching up workers' wounds. From there, he moved to the job of president of the Board of Pension Examining Surgeons. Well compensated by fees, he had no thoughts of taking another job.

Then a family friend, Mayor Cyrus P. Walbridge, came calling. Would Starkloff consider the job of health commissioner? No, Starkloff replied. Walbridge kept asking until Starkloff agreed in 1895. It would have been fair for him to have time to learn the tasks of abating health hazards and operating the city's hospitals that he had in the post, but first Starkloff had to deal with a smallpox epidemic. And when the sky darkened on the afternoon of May 27, 1896, his training was over. A gigantic tornado, the biggest in the city's history, roared through the city. When it was over, 255 people were dead and a thousand or so were injured. The wounded included Starkloff, whose arm was broken by a falling flagpole. Ignoring the excruciating pain he was in, Starkloff went forth to provide care for the wounded and dying. The most immediate need was at City Hospital, which was in the center of the path of the Great Cyclone of 1896. Within a day, about sixteen hundred patients at the hospital were moved to the Convent of the Good Shepherd. After all were safely in their quarters, he allowed doctors to treat his broken arm.

As health commissioner for most of the years from then until he retired in 1933, Starkloff became known around the country for much more than his untiring work in the cyclone and influenza epidemic. He helped St. Louis achieve one of the lowest infant death rates in the country, fought for clean milk, and campaigned for inoculation against diphtheria. A headline in the *St. Louis Globe-Democrat Magazine* in 1933 summed up his career this way: "St. Louis One of the Healthiest Spots in the United States." After he died in 1942, the city renamed its City Hospital south of downtown after him. At a dinner in Starkloff's honor at 1934, Kiel said, "I believe 'the Doc' has added many years to my life, probably to the lives of many of you here and of the people of St. Louis."

The Place for
Gemuetlichkeit

I n the years before America fought the Nazis and Japan, *Das Deutsche Haus* was the place for all things *Gemuetlichkeit*. Opened in 1929 after a campaign that included help from such German luminaries as former mayor Henry W. Kiel, it soon became a center of German-American life here. The four-story brick building at 2345 Lafayette Avenue was the home of seventy-six German societies within three years after it opened. Built for $380,000, it had meeting rooms and halls able to accommodate crowds from 40 to 1,200. The building was full of activity.

Carl Henne, a St. Louisan born in Germany, remembered those days in a 1972 article in the *St. Louis Globe-Democrat*. "It became the home for German-American societies—they all met before in the old Eagle Hall, which was right across the street," he said. "We had balls, dances, concerts and Christmas parties there. Every Sunday night we used to have a little German theater, too. The public Rathskeller in the basement and the bowling alley were good places just to drop in—there was always someone to talk to." He liked it so much that he chose it as the place for his wedding breakfast.

Then came the war, or at least the events leading to the war. In January 1939, word got out that Colin Ross, an agent for a Nazi publishing house in Germany, wanted to give a speech at the German House about the German occupation of the Sudetenland. Groups ranging from labor groups to the VFW to the American Legion to the St. Louis Council for American Democracy protested. Seeing the uproar, the board of directors of the German House turned the request down. Later, when the war started, the name was changed to the St. Louis House. Otherwise, though, it remained a place for Germans.

When the war ended, the name reverted to the German House. But times were different. People were leaving the city and didn't feel

The German House

safe in the neighborhood. Poor finances almost forced the place to close. Still, it remained a popular place for local German groups to have their offices and for events. "We had 800 people at our affair last fall," Henne, the president of the Schwaben Singing Society, said in a 1972 *Globe-Democrat* article. "If the neighborhood and parking get better again more German societies will go back—there's really no better place in town. The acoustics are great." The acoustics were so good that the St. Louis Symphony recorded an album at the German House, produced by Columbia Records. But the place wasn't good enough to survive just on Germans, and an owner said anyone who wanted to could use it. A Mexican bar and restaurant opened in the basement. The bowling alley closed. It was a matter of time before the place joined the ranks of shuttered German gathering places.

The German House was just one of the buildings Germans put up around St. Louis to gather for singing, dancing, exercising, arguing, or the theater. One was the Strassberger Music Conservatory. The three-story building at Grand Boulevard and Shenandoah Avenue once was a place to celebrate the city's German music culture after it was built in 1904–05. Today it has a mix of upscale apartments, offices, and stores.

Another building originally meant for a gathering place of Germans stands at 2930 North Twenty-first Street. In 1867, German settlers founded the *Freie Gemeinde*, or "Free Thinkers" Congregation. The building was home of a *Gesangverein* (choral club) and a library with three thousand books.

Some other buildings in the city formerly served as homes for Turner groups. They include the North St. Louis Turnverein, 1925 Mallinckrodt Street, and the South St. Louis Turnverein, 1519 South Tenth Street. One building that is home to a still-active group is the Concordia Turners, 6432 Gravois Avenue. But that's an exception. Almost all have a different purpose from the original German intent, and that includes the German House.

The end for the German House came in 1972, when the Gateway Temple of St. Louis, Inc. bought it for a church and school. In 2007, the Church of Scientology of Missouri bought the building for $1.6 million. Church officials plan to renovate the building, which would include a counseling area, classrooms, and an area for services. But for now, it's unused.

Irma Rombauer
Brings Joy

or more than eighty years, cooks in doubt have relied on the *Joy of Cooking* to keep their soufflés fluffed and their chocolate cupcakes moist. Some might conclude the volume had its beginning with a school for chefs or an East Coast cooking magazine. In fact, the first edition was produced in St. Louis by a fifty-four-year-old German-American widow named Irma Rombauer. "Joy" was in the title, but it was actually born in tragedy.

Rombauer's father was Dr. Max von Starkloff, a doctor who was born in Ulm, Germany, in 1832 and came to New York City in 1852. Some time before 1861, he arrived in the small town of Carondelet, south of St. Louis. Her mother was a German who came to St. Louis to help Susan Blow in her work to found America's first public kindergarten in Carondelet. The family became involved in the city's German social life. In 1889, President Benjamin Harrison named von Starkloff the U.S. Consul to Bremen in deference to his long service to the Republican Party. Before von Starkloff was replaced in 1894, Irma toured Germany extensively and developed a sense of German identity she never lost. In 1899, she married an up-and-coming young lawyer named Edgar Rombauer. Soon, she became a busy socialite and was involved in such groups as the Women's Symphony Society and the People's Art Center. That ended in 1930, when her husband died. The papers reported Edgar's death in a nondescript, matter-of-fact way, both at the time of his death and later in the 1960s when Irma died. In fact, the emotionally troubled lawyer committed suicide.

Suddenly, Irma Rombauer had bills to pay. Her recipes provided the answer. Her children coaxed her to start collecting the recipes she used for the memorable meals they'd had at home, along with ones from her travels. She badgered friends to add their own recipes and added stories, anecdotes, and tales from her three decades in the kitchen. Her daughter Marion provided illustrations and helped test recipes. She didn't bother finding a publisher but paid about three thousand dollars to have three thousand copies printed herself.

The book she sold from her home at 5712 Cabanne Avenue was an immediate success. "In *The Joy of Cooking*, Mrs. Rombauer successfully imparts the feeling that cooking never is nor should be a dull task," Marguerite Martyn wrote in a review in the *St. Louis Post-Dispatch*. "Though a thoroughly practical cook book, well indexed and including old and honored recipes as well as the newest fads and fancies, there is not a dull page in it," Martyn wrote. "Her directions were clear and easy to follow." With her self-published book a success, Rombauer started searching for a publisher. She revised and enlarged her book and fine-tuned it. In 1936, Bobbs-Merrill published it.

Sales were fair but not earth-shattering. Everything changed in 1943, when Rombauer revised the book and combined it with *Streamlined Cooking,* a book she published in 1939. Sales of the new improved *Joy*

of Cooking took off and never stopped. She was embarrassed when sales of that book topped the best-seller list and eclipsed *One World*, the book by Wendell Willkie, the 1940 Republican candidate for president. So she sent Willkie a copy of the book with her "sincere apologies" on the flyleaf. "I have scanned it carefully," Willkie's wife wrote, "and can truthfully say it is the most interesting cook book I ever read."

Her daughter, then Marion Rombauer Becker, joined her in later years as a co-author. The book kept selling even after Irma Rombauer's death in 1962 and the death of her daughter in 1976. Today, it's still in print. The latest edition—published in 2006—celebrated the book's seventy-fifth anniversary. It featured updates and revisions provided by Rombauer's grandson Ethan Becker, his wife Susan, and Maggie Green, a dietician and nutritionist. Altogether, it has 4,500 recipes, including 500 new ones and 4,000 updated and retested classics. It's much different from the first book, which was written in a time when housewives scoured kitchen knives with lemon juice to prevent staining and boxes full of ice were used by most people to keep food cold. Besides Rombauer's original recipes, the book contains advice on such modern treats as pizza with grilled eggplant, mushrooms, and sun-dried tomatoes. One thing remains the same. Then and now, the book kept the joy in cooking.

The End of the Last German Paper

hen the *Westliche Post* closed in September 1938, many blamed the Depression, high taxes, newsprint prices, and even the debate over Nazism among the area's German-Americans. The truth was the German-language paper suspended publication because assimilation worked. Few spoke German anymore. But for 103 years—81 for the *Westliche Post*—German-language papers in St. Louis had some of the most vibrant writing. The *Post* and the *Anzeiger des Westens* were the most notable German-language papers in St. Louis, but they were hardly the only ones. In the early period, for example, the *Tages-Chronik* stood firmly for Catholicism, while the *Deutsche Tribuene* spoke out for the Whig Party. Nine German-language newspapers were listed in Kennedy's St. Louis Directory in 1860, although some of them actually were supplements. The spirit of the often-feisty German-language press is honored in St. Louis's Reservoir Park, where the Naked Truth monument notes the contributions of *Westliche Post* editors Carl Daenzer, Emil Preetorius, and Carl Schurz.

The *Westliche Post* was born when Daenzer quit his job as editor of the *Anzeiger des Westens* in 1857 to start the *Post*. By 1860, mentally and physically exhausted, he went to Europe. Two years later, his health revived, he returned to St. Louis. Seeing that the *Anzeiger des Westens* had folded, he brought it back to life. Then in 1864, the *Westliche Post* merged with *Die Neue Zeit*. With the merger, *Die Neue Zeit* editor Emil Preetorius became editor of the *Westliche Post*. Preetorius left Germany following the failed revolution of 1848 and arrived in St. Louis in 1853. In 1867, the paper got a new investor, Carl Schurz, who served as a general in the Civil War and later as a senator from Missouri. But for the moment, he was content to serve as co-editor with Preetorius of the *Westliche Post*.

The biggest accomplishment of the two came in a game of chess.

While playing at the Mercantile Library Hall, Schurz and Preetorius encountered an immigrant from Hungary named Joseph Pulitzer. He impressed them so much that they hired him for a reporting job in 1868. Pulitzer became part owner of the paper by 1871 but sold his share in 1873 and founded the *St. Louis Post-Dispatch* in 1878. Five years later, Pulitzer bought the *New York World* and started remaking journalism.

In 1898, the operations of the *Anzeiger des Westens* and the *Westliche Post* were combined. The German-American Press Association published the *Post* in the morning and for a while the *Anzeiger des Westens* in the evening. The *Anzeiger* died in 1912, not long before the *Westliche Post* found itself in a controversy over its stance on World War I. When the war started, the *Post* was strongly in favor of Germany, but after the United States entered the conflict, it supported the draft and promoted the sale of Liberty Bonds. When members of the French mission visited St. Louis in May 1917, the paper advised Germans not to commit any affronts against them.

After the war ended, the next big enemy of the *Westliche Post* was the Depression. It didn't stop members of the St. Louis Advertising Club from celebrating the seventy-fifth anniversary of the newspaper in March 1932 by singing "*Schnitzelbank*" and eating sauerkraut and pretzels at the Hotel Statler. The next year, workers celebrated after being allowed to take over ownership of the paper after assuming about $26,000 in debt. This was no workers' paradise. As costs increased, the *Post* missed a daily edition on June 6, 1938, for the first time since 1857. Nine days later, it announced that henceforth it would publish a fattened Sunday paper and drop all other editions. It wasn't enough to save the paper. On September 11, 1938, with its money exhausted, the *Westliche Post* printed its last edition. At the end, circulation was just above fifteen thousand papers a day. The brewing conflict in Germany didn't help. The paper stayed neutral toward the Nazi Party. Nazis accused the *Post* of being communist. Opponents said the paper was run by Nazis. That didn't matter to those mourning its loss. "A German-language newspaper, it has been said that it spoke German with a St. Louis accent since it was solidly of, for and by St. Louis," the *Post-Dispatch* editorialized. "But its constituency thinned as result of the steady decline of the German-speaking population."

The Unwilling Guests of War

he burial ceremony on October 24, 1944, was as good as any held for a German soldier at the height of World War II. Uniformed mourners stood at attention at the funeral of Gustav Pfarrer and raised the Nazi salute. What made it different was that the funeral wasn't in Germany, but at Jefferson Barracks National Cemetery in south St. Louis County. In fighting at Anzio, Italy, Pfarrer lost his right arm and was captured. On an army train headed for an Oklahoma hospital, he became sick near St. Louis and died at the Jefferson Barracks post hospital. The soldiers attending his burial were prisoners of war. He was one of two German POWs buried at Jefferson Barracks. The other was Sergeant Max Suemnick, who died on June 29, 1944.

As David Fiedler related in his book, *The Enemy Among Us: POWs in Missouri During World War II,* prisoners and captors often developed warm relations. With American workers overseas fighting, POWs repaired army vehicles, worked on farms, and patched shoes. They even enjoyed Sunday trips to the Fox Theater. Altogether, fifteen thousand prisoners of war stayed at twenty POW camps in Missouri in World War II. Five camps were in the St. Louis area, Chesterfield and Jefferson Barracks among them.

Just before Christmas 1944, the *St. Louis Star-Times* sent a reporter to the Jefferson Barracks POW camp to report on how Uncle Sam was treating his Nazi guests. Just fine, reporter Harry Wohl stated: "While the Nazis scorn the most basic rights of the people they have subjugated, German prisoners of war at Jefferson Barracks make sure that their own rights are respected, the *Star-Times* found during a tour of their compound." Wohl offered that prisoners were ready with copies of the Geneva Convention, which places limits on their treatment. "But they need have no fear: Uncle Sam plays strictly according to Hoyle."

Photos with the article showed a prisoner wearing a white cook's jacket decorating a birthday cake while others removed eyes from pota-toes already scraped clean by a machine. The food, savory and tasty, was as good as soldiers received in base camp. POWs were allowed to write one letter a week to relatives. Prisoners, mostly members of Rommel's Afrika Korps who had been captured in Tunisia, received 80 cents a day for a workday that began at 8 a.m. and ended at 4:30 p.m. Musicians formed an orchestra, complete with bass violas, accordions, violins, clarinet, and piano. One young-looking pianist was playing Beethoven as a reporter walked by. "The pianist paused for a moment in apparent embarrassment, then changed to a lusty tune filled with defiance," Wohl wrote.

About 540 German prisoners lived at Jefferson Barracks, said Marc Kollbaum, curator at St. Louis County's Jefferson Barracks Historic Park. Some did maintenance work at Jefferson Barracks, some were janitors at war plants, while others toiled at truck farms nearby.

The POWs at Jefferson Barracks only once caused serious problems. It happened on January 18, 1945, when three hundred to four hundred POWs stopped work after a prisoner was disciplined. Not willing to negotiate with the strikers, authorities jailed them on a diet of bread and water. The strike collapsed and gave newshawks something to write about, but it never endangered Americans. Neither did the escape of two former German corporals from the agricultural labor camp barracks in Chesterfield on the rainy night of October 21, 1945. Joseph Swoboda and Michael Kunz, who had been working at Hellwig Brothers' truck farm near Chesterfield, left a note: "Maybe we don't have a chance. Nevertheless we will try. We say who doesn't risk can't win." The risk failed. On October 30, they were picked up while hitchhiking near Waterloo, Illinois. In broken English, they said they were cold, tired, and hungry and wanted to return to their camp. Their plan to go to South America fell apart when they got lost.

Their hopes to go home, however, succeeded. In 1946, camps at Chesterfield, Jefferson Barracks, and many other places were deactivated. The POWs left, but memories remained. As Fiedler noted, they weren't always negative: "They came as our enemy, but in many cases they left as friends or, at the least, with a more positive view of the United States."

Pastor to the
Unforgivable

After ministering to prisoners in the St. Louis City Workhouse, the Reverend Henry Gerecke was used to bringing the gospel into jails. But nothing could prepare this German-American Lutheran minister for the assignment he had after World War II. The South Side preacher became spiritual confidante for some of the worst Nazis to survive World War II: Hermann Goering, Albert Speer, Joachim Von Ribbentrop, and others. His ministry to fifteen hated Protestant defendants during the Nuremberg trials brought meaning to the notion that God forgives everyone.

Gerecke brought to the assignment an upbringing in a farm family that spoke both German and English. Born in Gordonville, Missouri, he was the son of a man who emigrated from Hanover, Germany. After attending Concordia Seminary in St. Louis, he was ordained in 1926 and was named pastor of Christ Lutheran Church in South St. Louis. In 1935, he was named executive director of the St. Louis Lutheran City Mission at Tenth Street and Cass Avenue. As leader of a church's work that went into nursing homes, hospitals, schools, and jails, Gerecke worked regularly with the unchurched and unsavable. In the city workhouse, he preached to murderers as well as shoplifters. "Show them Jesus, Savior from sin" was the advice he gave workers at his mission. He brought his message to shut-ins and the hospitalized in *Moments of Comfort*, his weekly program on the Lutheran radio station KFUO.

When war started he could have relied on his age to keep him in his comfortable home at 3204 Halliday Avenue. Instead, he entered the Chaplains School at Harvard University. He was pastor to the wounded in Great Britain from March 1944 to June 1945 before coming to France. Then he visited the Dachau concentration camp, "where my hand, touching a wall, was smeared with the human blood seeping through." It was enough to make him dread his next assignment. Gerecke was a Lutheran, had ministered in prisons, and spoke German. With that background, his superiors offered him the post of chaplain to Protestants on trial for war crimes at Nuremberg. It would be an unpopular job and his age could keep him out of it. But he accepted. "Slowly the men at Nuremberg became to me just lost souls whom I was being asked to help," he wrote.

Prisoners responded differently to Gerecke's appeals to attend the first Sunday service in November 1945. Former *Luftwaffe* chief Hermann Goering said he would, but Gerecke thought he just wanted a chance to get out of his cell. He found Field Marshall Wilhelm Keitel reading a Bible and professing God could even love a sinner like him. In the end, thirteen of the fifteen Protestant defendants attended his first service. In time, he gave communion to seven of the fifteen, after he became convinced they had repented.

The work continued until late spring 1946, when rumors spread among the inmates: Gerecke's wife wanted him home. One day, his wife received a letter with this message: "We have now heard, dear Mrs. Gerecke, that you wish to see (your husband) back home. . . . we understand this wish very well. Nevertheless we are asking you to put off your wish to gather your family around you," the letter said. "Our dear Chaplain Gerecke is necessary for us, not only as a pastor, but as the thoroughly good man that he is." It was signed by all Catholics and Protestants at Nuremberg. Alma Gerecke sent the message, "They need you."

So Gerecke stayed with the defendants until verdicts came back. Eleven were sentenced to death. Goering denied the Christian faith but nonetheless asked for communion. Gerecke refused. "I could not grant the Lord's supper to a man denying the divinity of the Savior who instituted this rite," he said. Before his scheduled execution, Goering killed himself by swallowing potassium cyanide he had hidden. Others professed their faith. "I place all my confidence in the Lamb who made atonement for my sins. May God have mercy on my soul," former German foreign minister Joachim Von Ribbentrop declared.

His work done, Gerecke came home in November 1946. He served as an Army prison chaplain until 1950, when he was named joint pastor of St. John Lutheran Church in Chester, Illinois. He also served prisoners at the Menard State Penitentiary in Illinois until he died in 1961. Senders of hate mail condemned him as a "Jew hater." To this, his son, Henry H. Gerecke, offered a different reason in a 2000 article in the *St. Louis Post-Dispatch*. "He didn't choose the job, but he felt God wanted him to do it."

Henry Gerecke

Pastor to the Nuremberg defendants

School Sisters of Notre Dame, St. Liborius

Matters of Faith

A New Promised Land

our years after Americans took charge in St. Louis, an ad appeared in the village's new newspaper, the *Missouri Gazette*, on November 9, 1808. "Jacob Philipson has just received, and is now opening at his new store, opposite the post-office, a seasonable supply of dry goods, and a general assortment of groceries." Jacob Philipson's brother Joseph had arrived in St. Louis late in 1807. As far as anybody knows, Joseph Philipson was the first Jew in the little village. Jacob apparently came soon after, and Simon followed later.

Germany figured in their lives before they arrived in the United States in the late 1790s or early 1800s, but how much is a matter of disagreement. They were born in a part of Poland that later was taken over by Prussia. Some say they were Polish Jews, but others claimed the words "Polish Jews" and "German Jews" both were used for people who came from parts of Germany that had been part of Poland. Evidently, they were in Hamburg before they came to America. In St. Louis, the Philipsons prospered. Joseph made beer under the name "St. Louis Brewery" and owned a sawmill. He taught piano and possessed a library that included *The Tragedies of Faust*, volumes of Anastasis in Italian, and scientific books. After Joseph Philipson died in 1844, many of the city's most distinguished citizens came to his funeral.

Other German Jews followed as the city's population burgeoned, but their numbers were small. Weary about his health, Louis Krafter committed suicide in St. Louis in August 1839. With no Jewish cemeteries in St. Louis, he was buried in Cincinnati. The rapid influx of new residents in the 1840s and 1850s brought numerous Jews, and congregations to serve them. Many German Jews downplayed their

Judaism in their desire to become fully American. Some joined liberal Reform congregations, while others ceased practicing Judaism.

German Jews in St. Louis were targets of bigotry, as Catholics and other immigrants were, but they survived and prospered. As with Jews everywhere, their arrival added to the business, civic, and cultural life of their new home. German Jews were at the center of numerous charitable efforts, including the drive to start the Jewish Hospital of St. Louis. That hospital became part of the world-renowned Barnes-Jewish-Christian (BJC) hospital network in 1996.

Business and merchandising were the paths to success for a number of German Jews in St. Louis. They had their hands in such companies as Stix, Baer & Fuller as well as Famous-Barr. One German businessman, Jacob D. Goldman, was born in Essenheim, Germany, and emigrated to America at the age of fifteen in 1860. He moved to Georgia, joined the 54th Georgia Infantry Regiment during the Civil War, and arrived in St. Louis at the war's end. Cotton companies he helped found were major forces in making St. Louis a prime mover in the cotton business.

A German-Jewish businessman made a public declaration of his faith that survives today. The cornerstone of the building Marcus Bernheimer erected for his business at 702 N. Second Street on the riverfront notes it was laid in 1883 but also includes the Jewish year 5644. The son of a Prussian mother and an Austrian father, he was raised in Mississippi, fought for the Confederacy, and came to St. Louis in 1875. He made his money in the wholesale grocery business, a Meramec River resort, and flour manufacturing. He lost the race for the Democratic nomination for St. Louis mayor in 1893, but he was elected St. Louis circuit clerk in 1910 and kept the job until he died in 1912.

Business may have made others well known, but Jacob Mahler danced to success. The son of a German dance master and musician, he was born in Chicago in 1858. After his father established a dance academy in St. Louis, he became proficient at age four and a teacher at eleven. He long led the grand march at the Veiled Prophet balls and taught queens and their courts the finer ways of walking and bowing. But new dances and jazz scandalized Mahler. To him, trendy new dances like the turkey trot and the grizzly bear were mere "rags." He refused to teach the fox trot until the demand was overwhelming. Three years before he died in 1928, he appeared in a revue at the Mahler Dancing Academy that included the dreaded fox trot. The master knew when it was time to give in to the new ways.

A Survivor's Good Life

udy Oppenheim's mother wanted to leave Germany in 1931, two years before Adolf Hitler came to power. She didn't leave, but after the two nights of anti-Jewish violence on November 9 and 10, 1938, known as *Kristallnacht*, Oppenheim's parents and others in his family realized there was no more time for delay and left for Shanghai, China. Twenty-six members of his extended family who didn't leave died. After two years, the family came to the United States and settled in the St. Louis area.

At eighty-three, Oppenheim tells the story from the perspective of a life well lived. He made his living as a chemist and spent forty years as president of Chevra Kadisha Ohave Sholom, a congregation of German-Jewish refugees who fled the Nazis. He has four children, eight grandchildren, and four great-grandchildren. As of March 2012, two more great-grandchildren were on the way. Photos of Oppenheim with his family and his congregation are featured in a display on St. Louis–area holocaust survivors at the St. Louis Holocaust Museum and Learning Center.

Rudy Oppenheim was ten in 1938, young enough to see what happened as an adventure. The Jews in Shanghai bought old school buildings, where they lived twenty-four to a room. Although conditions were crowded, they were well fed and able to find jobs. There were so many German Jews that the Chinese grocers in the area learned to speak German. In 1940, the family came to America and lived in Granite City, Illinois. There, Oppenheim's father, a chemist who worked in leather degreasing, worked for Smith-Roland Co. Three years later, the Oppenheims moved to St. Louis.

Things were not easy for the Oppenheims and other German Jews who had come to America. They sought to help the American cause and were willing to fight, work in defense plants, or do any other task that would help defeat the Nazis. "The German Jew had to fend for himself," Oppenheim said in a 2004 interview. Those German Jews banded together as soon as they escaped Nazi persecution and came to St. Louis. As Jews kept coming from Germany, the group worked to find them jobs and places to live. In the evenings, they met in the former Young Men's Hebrew Association building on Union Boulevard to receive instruction in German on the American way of life. Others learned English in what came to be known as night school. At its height, the group had eight hundred to nine hundred members.

In 1937, German Jews founded Chevra Kadisha Ohave Sholomand and held religious services of their own for Yom Kippur, the Day of Atonement, and Rosh Hashanah, the Jewish New Year, at the Berger Memorial Funeral Home at 4700 McPherson Avenue in St. Louis. Manfred Isenberg, a professional cantor trained in the methods of rabbis, gave sermons in German. The songs were alive with German harmony. In time, members of the Chevra who had children joined synagogues with Sunday School and Hebrew Schools. The services for High Holy Days kept on until 1964.

The Chevra declined over the years. Today, it has about twenty-eight members. But the heritage of the organization lives on in a tiny cemetery at 7400 Olive Boulevard. Just eighty-eight by ninety-one feet,

Rudy Oppenheim

it was originally acquired by the Brith Sholom Congregation in 1932 as a cemetery plot. Later, the German Jews expressed interest because they wanted to be together in death as they had been in life. They bought the property with the idea of putting a synagogue in front and the cemetery behind. The synagogue was never built, but the cemetery was dedicated in 1949. Gravestones pointed east face a granite monument honoring the Jewish victims of Nazi persecution. Eventually, a Jewish community center was built behind the cemetery. Today, the Agape Academy and Child Development Center, a Christian school, occupies that building.

All 258 gravesites in the cemetery are either taken or accounted for. Those buried in the cemetery include Oppenheim's parents, his brother, and his grandmother. Oppenheim himself is a former president of the cemetery. He finds time for work in the Jewish community, including speaking about survivors of Nazi rule. He has been to Germany three times and has spoken to Germans about his experiences. Once he talked about his past in an address to four hundred students in his hometown of Elmshorn, Germany. "They asked me, 'Do you hate us?' I said, 'How can I hate you? You're a different generation,'" Oppenheim said. "You cannot live with hate."

A German Church in Frenchtown

oday, the Soulard neighborhood is known for its rousing Mardi Gras celebration, an event tied to French Catholics and New Orleans. The neighborhood got its name from Antoine Soulard, a Frenchman who surveyed the area for the King of Spain. With its French farmers, locals called the area Frenchtown, but it was anything but French at the end of the 1840s. When census takers finished their 1850 count in the city's First Ward—south of Chouteau and east of Seventeenth Street—they found two-thirds of the population was German.

Many Germans in the First Ward, which included Frenchtown, were Lutherans, but a large number were underserved Catholics. The city's two German parishes—St. Mary of Victories and St. Joseph—were north of the ward. St. Vincent de Paul Church, the only Catholic Church in the ward, was meant both for Irish and German immigrants. Archbishop Richard Kenrick knew this couldn't go on. In 1849, he assigned a German priest, Simon Sigrist, to organize the parish of Sts. Peter and Paul. For more than a century following, priests at the church would continue to give some of their sermons in German.

The parish found a parcel of land for a small frame church and rectory at Eighth Street and Allen Avenue, where the current church is located. Classes for the parish school were held at a nearby home. The tiny church wasn't big enough for the two thousand souls counted in the 1851 parish census. A larger building opened in 1853.

If there was a time and place when German Catholics needed a spiritual sanctuary, it was at Sts. Peter and Paul Parish in the 1850s. Protestant Know-Nothings and Irish Catholics from North St. Louis battled members of the church in taverns and streets. The original French residents of the area also opposed them. Sigrist's sermons had the stuff to rouse his downtrodden flock, but as church debt grew, some criticized him for his inability to handle finances. In 1858, Kenrick tired of the infighting and replaced him with his assistant, Father Franz de Sales Goller. He got it right the second time.

Born in Westphalia, Germany, Goller attended seminary in Germany and the University of Tuebingen. His work at Sts. Peter and Paul showed he was a talented administrator worthy of advancement. He was held back after 1868, when Kenrick stopped promoting German priests. To preserve German traditions and to keep the Catholic faith, Goller fought to keep the German language and against assimilation. He also worried about Protestants who thought Catholic immigrants were more devoted to the Pope than the United States.

As one way to preserve the German-Catholic tradition, Goller asked the School Sisters of Notre Dame to help at the parish school. Three sisters from the teaching order that started in Germany were ready to teach two hundred students when an expanded school opened in a new building on Eighth Street in 1859. It grew to more than seven hundred in 1869 and more than thirteen hundred by 1900. Two hundred boys also attended a boys' high school established in 1866. He also opened a parish hall in 1871 to provide members of Sts. Peter and Paul with a place for social life.

As the parish grew, Goller called on the German-American architect Franz Georg Himpler to design a proper German Gothic Church. It was dedicated in 1875, complete with statues and stained glass windows showing the German influence. Seriously damaged in the monstrous tornado of 1896, the church was quickly repaired. Happy with the refurbished church, Goller lived to celebrate his fiftieth anniversary in the parish in 1905 with a torchlight parade and praise from throughout America. He died five years later.

Goller saw to it that worshippers sang hymns in German at the 8 a.m. Sunday Mass and that people could confess their sins to a priest in German. But, inevitably, assimilation won. Urban decline set in. The parish school closed in 1967, fifty-three years after the high school shut down in 1914. Then, as with much of the South Side, came a restoration of the parish. Today, a diverse group of worshippers, many from outside the parish boundaries, calls Sts. Peter and Paul home. Its ministries to the homeless and needy are different from the ones the original parishioners chose, but members only have to look around their sanctuary to see evidence of their parish's German heritage.

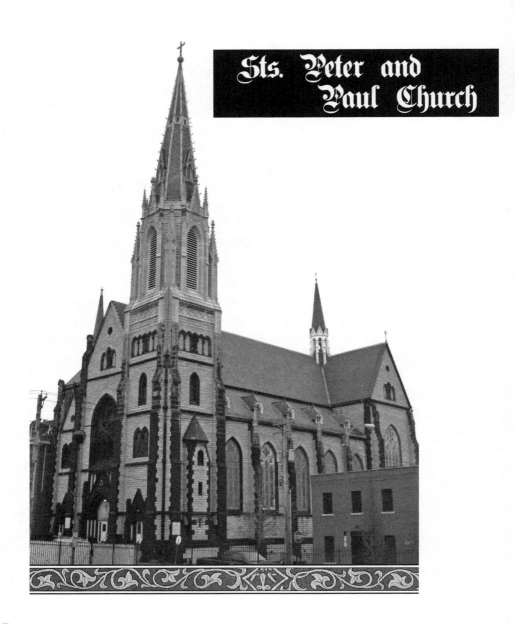

Sts. Peter and Paul Church

The Great German-Irish Catholic Donnybrook

hen members of St. Francis de Sales Catholic Parish laid the cornerstone for a new church in 1895, Catholics throughout the city marked the occasion with a parade to end all parades. Germans, Poles, and Bohemians all turned out for the fete for the church at Gravois and Ohio avenues. But the Irish stayed away from the beginning of what became known as the Cathedral of the South Side. The story of why that happened goes back half a century.

For decades, Irish and German Catholics fought over whether it was better to assimilate quickly into American Catholic culture or to remain separate in "national" churches until they gradually fit in. The war waged wherever Catholic Irish and German immigrants lived close by, but St. Louis seemed to be the epicenter. The Catholic German clergy worried about the masses of immigrants coming into the United States. Their solution was to protect them from abandoning their faith and cultural identity by establishing separate German-speaking organizations, parochial schools and churches. They saw it as a way to protect Germans against American Protestants who thought Catholic immigrants were more devoted to the Pope than America. And they believed it was a way to protect their flocks against such heathen Germans as newspaper editor Heinrich Boernstein, whose work included the outrageously anti-Catholic *Mysteries of St. Louis; Or, the Jesuits on the Prairie des Noyers, A Western Tale.*

The roots of the controversy date to 1845, when Bishop Peter Richard Kenrick started a system to allow separate immigrant churches—including German ones—within other parishes. Some resented the policy, particularly Irish immigrants. Their reasons weren't just theological. Irish and Germans competed for the same jobs. Germans tended to be Republicans while more Irish voted Democratic. The Irish leaned toward the French during the Franco-Prussian War, and the Germans naturally favored the Prussians. While Germans brewed the beer, they may have looked down at the raucous way the Irish consumed it.

It was natural that the English-speaking Irish were more comfortable blending in with Americans than people of a foreign tongue. The Irish argued for rapid assimilation while holding on to Catholic ways. Wary of German Catholic nationalism, the historian John Gilmary called it "a canker eating away at the life of the church in the United States."

Such talk reminded the Germans of the Know-Nothings, the nativists who lashed out against Irish and German immigrants in the 1840s and 1850s. They complained about a lack of opportunity for advancement for German priests. Indeed, after the Civil War, eight Irish priests from St. Louis became bishops, but only one German priest reached such a high level. Germans also claimed that the churches set up under Kenrick's 1845 order weren't really independent and equal.

Those who fought for assimilation called themselves Americanizers. They developed a word—complete with an "ism" at the end—for those who opposed them. The word was "Cahenslyism" for Peter Paul Cahensly. A member of the Centre Party of the German Reichstag, Cahensly was president of the St. Raphael's Society, a group set up to guide German immigrants to America to places where they could make a living and hold on to their faith.

Some saw Cahensly as part of a German government conspiracy to Germanize the American church, but all indications are that Cahensly's interests were not nationalistic but a desire to help German Catholics in America. In time, Irish Catholics agreed. It helped that Kenrick issued a decree in 1896 that all immigrant parishes were equal and independent from all other churches. Germans could be as separate as they desired without worrying about attacks from other groups, but nothing could stop them from blending in with American society.

Teachers from Bavaria

 other Caroline Friess was aghast at her pupils. "To try to discipline such was no mean task. They sat in their seats with arms akimbo, legs stretched one over the other. One wanted to read, another to write and still another to knit," she wrote. "They seem, so to say, to hate the German. One only hears the English language spoken here." But she had a solution. "They must be led to good with earnestness and firmness but with all the love one can show them. This is a very difficult task and one that needs a special help from God."

Mother Caroline was used to seeking help from God. She was a member of the School Sisters of Notre Dame, an educational religious order founded in Bavaria in 1833. In 1847, a group of six from the order came to America in response to a call by American bishops to help teach children of German immigrants. In 1858, Mother Caroline brought a sister, two novices, and a candidate for the sisterhood to St. Louis to educate children at the German parish of St. Joseph on Biddle Street. Quickly, they were teaching more than two hundred children. Some pupils chafed at the sisters' insistence on High German and strict discipline, but the sisters didn't budge and eventually won out.

Their efforts soon expanded to other schools, often at great sacrifice. Sisters who taught at Sts. Peter and Paul School in Soulard lived at the top floor of the parish convent, sweltering through St. Louis summers without modern conveniences like air conditioning or even fans. When they came to St. Liborius—also called the "Northside Cathedral"—in 1859, the sisters taught at first without the benefit of a school building. Instead, they used two rooms in the rectory as classrooms. This required more sacrifice from the sisters and from the church's pastor, the Reverend Stephen Schweihoff, an immigrant from the diocese of Paderborn, Germany. He slept among the vestments

School Sisters of Notre Dame

Mother Caroline

in the church sacristy. The sisters, meanwhile, stayed at Sts. Peter and Paul. When he could, a helpful gentleman named Amend took them to St. Liborius. Otherwise, they walked. It wasn't long before they offered their help to children of other immigrant groups. In 1869, for example, Mother Caroline opened the first Czech Catholic School in America at St. John Nepomuk Church on Bohemian Hill.

Eventually, the School Sisters of Notre Dame taught in hundreds of parochial schools and dozens of high schools and academies, from Jefferson City to Effingham, Poplar Bluff to Milwaukee. By the time she died in 1892, Mother Caroline had established 265 schools in the United States and Canada. Before her death, Mother Caroline asked for the establishment of a new St. Louis Province, with its headquarters at a motherhouse in St. Louis.

Two years after her death, the order bought a twenty-one-acre estate in present-day Lemay called Grand View. It came complete with a resplendent view of the Mississippi and a dwelling—called the White House—which the sisters occupied until the larger motherhouse was built. Mother Bonaventure Wagner brought six sisters to the place on March 15, 1895, and began work on creating a center for educational and spiritual development of new members. They called it Sancta Maria in Ripa (St. Mary on the Bank). But when soldiers at the nearby Jefferson Barracks talked about the place, they spoke of "The German Sisters on the Hill." For although it was nearly forty years since they had arrived in St. Louis, they kept the German language as part of their everyday life. When the cornerstone was laid for the motherhouse, sermons were given in English and German.

The motherhouse itself was dedicated in July 1897. Ten years later, work began on an addition. While they had long since expanded from their original focus of teaching German immigrants, the School Sisters of Notre Dame retained their interest in things German. They said prayers in German until World War I and even sent "Care Packages" to members of their order in Germany during World War II.

After World War II, they spread throughout twenty states, plus Ghana, Honduras, Japan, Kenya, Korea, Nepal, Nigeria, and Puerto Rico. The number of School Sisters has since dwindled. The Lemay campus—which also hosts the all-girls Notre Dame High School—once was home to three hundred sisters, and now numbers just one hundred. It is the location of the provincial offices for the Central Pacific Province, which consists of the former Milwaukee, St. Louis, Dallas, and Mankato, Minnesota, provinces. A tiny group of sisters from Bavaria came to America to teach the children of German immigrants, and their hard work and perseverance have educated a substantial portion of St. Louis and beyond.

A Fateful Meeting

plaque is mounted at the entrance to St. Johns Evangelical United Church of Christ in Mehlville. It notes that on October 15, 1840, six pastors from Germany who met on the property formed the Deutsche Evangelische Kirchenverein des Westens, or the German Evangelical Church Society of the West. The church wasn't the first congregation of its kind in the St. Louis area. The oldest was the German Protestant Evangelical Church of the Holy Spirit in St. Louis, which was formed in 1834 and was one of the six churches represented at the 1840 meeting. The meeting had major consequences still felt throughout the 1.2-million-member United Church of Christ.

The meeting was held after the Reverend Louis Ernst Nollau, pastor of St. Johns, sent a letter to evangelical pastors in the area asking them to meet with him to discuss ways to work together. Pastors from Holy Spirit, Femme Osage, St. Charles in Missouri, and Quincy and Centerville (now Millstadt) in Illinois joined Nollau. From that meeting came a union of German churches in the St. Louis area that eventually became part of the United Church of Christ. Today, anyone who joins a very old church of that denomination in the St. Louis area generally becomes part of a congregation once associated with that early union of German churches. Most likely, German was the main language spoken in those churches at the start of the twentieth century.

The group that started at St. Johns in 1840 traced itself to the forced union of the Lutheran and Reformed faiths in the German Evangelical Church of the Prussian Union in 1817. The organization continued and became the German Evangelical Synod of the West in 1866. In 1872, it combined with two other groups and became the German Evangelical Synod of North America. That church body dropped the word *German* in 1925, when the German language was disappearing in many congregations. The Evangelical Synod of North

America combined with the Reformed Church in the United States in 1934 to create the Evangelical and Reformed Church. That group's merger with the Association of Congregational Christian Churches in 1957 created the United Church of Christ. Many churches that began in the German Evangelical Synod of North America kept the word *Evangelical* in their names to show their heritage.

St. Johns is among those churches that still have *Evangelical* in its name. It began with a reluctant pastor. Nollau had no intention to minister to German farmers outside St. Louis. He was headed to Oregon, where he wanted to be a missionary to Indians. But on his way west, he lay over in St. Louis and heard an appeal to serve immigrants in the Gravois settlement, at present-day Mehlville. In the home of Adam Theiss, they organized the Deutsche Evangelische St. Johannes Gemeinde Zu Gravois Settlement Missouri in 1838. Members met in Heinrich Mueller's barn until they built a log church in 1839 on land donated by Christian Crecelius and Jonas Mueller.

In the years after the 1840 meeting, St. Johns followed the path of other evangelical churches that became part of the UCC. Like sister churches in the area, St. Johns experienced the decline of the German culture and language early in the twentieth century. Meetings were held in German at St. Johns until 1912, when members voted to have a service in English one evening a month. Today, the church's ninety-year-old building—its third—occupies the same property as the original. Urban sprawl long ago overwhelmed this once-rural church, and its congregation no longer is exclusively German. But like the original church, St. Johns still serves its members and its community.

The Church That Wasn't a Church

he Free Congregation of New Bremen acted like a church,
except for a small detail. The congregation, known to
local Germans as *Die Freie Gemeinde von Nord-St. Louis*,
was a church without religion. Dedicated to the gospel of
rationalism that flourished at the beginning of the nineteenth century in
Germany, it had a major influence in North St. Louis until around World
War I. It counted among its influential members the editors of two
German-language newspapers, Heinrich Boernstein of the *Anzeiger des
Westens* and Emil Preetorius of the *Westliche Post*. It continued until the
1970s, when the handful of remaining members and money went to the
Ethical Society, a group that most resembled the Free Congregation of
New Bremen.

The congregation grew from the Society of Free Men, which was
established in the late 1840s in Bremen, a German community in what
now is North St. Louis. From that society came a "free independent
church," officially known as the German School Society and Free
Congregation of St. Louis and Bremen. The organization founded a
German school to fill an educational vacuum in the area. Founders
emphasized that morality would be taught. Preaching would be based
on logic and would be free of any kind of religious indoctrination. God
wasn't totally excluded, as long as he was considered in a way members
thought was logical. The purpose of meetings was "cognition of truth,
restoring of the common feeling to truly do our duties, strengthening of
brotherly community life."

The Free Congregation, however, wasn't just a nice congregation
that happened to downplay religion. It was part of a movement
of German freethinkers in St. Louis that seemed intent on making
life miserable for people with a strong faith in God. In 1839, the

antireligious German-language St. Louis newspaper *Anzeiger des Westens* filled its pages with anything negative it could find about the arrival of about 750 traditionalist Lutherans led by Martin Stephan. Jesuits were favorite targets of freethinkers. Boernstein, for example, made Jesuits to seem like cheap gangsters pulling the strings in his laughably anti-Catholic novel, *The Mysteries of St. Louis*. No wonder F. A. Gottschalk, the congregation's first president, ended the church's first annual meeting on January 4, 1851, by urging all to support the antireligious German press in "opposing the assaults of priesthood and Jesuitism."

In 1852, the church called Carl Luedeking as speaker, a position more or less the same as pastor. Although he didn't always hold that position in the congregation, he had a major influence in the church until he died in 1885. A former Evangelical theology student, he had come to New York in 1851 after he aroused the displeasure of the government and church in his native land of Hessia. He stepped down as speaker in 1853 but recalled that time in an address he gave at the dedication of a new church assembly hall in 1867. "The year and a half which I at that time spent in this environment belong to the most beautiful, because they were the most fruitful and intellectually stimulating of my life." He ended his speech by calling Free Congregations bulwarks of consistency, places for reason and justice, and beacons of truth.

Other speakers followed, including Rudolph Doehn, who became a regimental chaplain at the start of the Civil War. When Doehn assumed the post of chaplain, Luedeking became an unpaid lecturer for the Free Congregation. In 1869, Luedeking served as the only delegate of Free Congregations in North America at the World Freethinkers' Congress in Naples, Italy. The meeting was not just a time for fellowship, but also a response to the Ecumenical Council held at the Vatican in 1869 and 1870. Those at that council spoke out against rationalism, materialism, and atheism and declared the doctrine of papal infallibility.

Back home, the congregation's school closed in 1869. Members reasoned that since the city schools now taught German in a strongly secular environment, there was no need for a separate school. In the years to come, the congregation raised money for a German orphanage, made a contribution for victims of a flood in Germany, and sponsored a festival in 1889 marking the one hundredth anniversary of the first inauguration of George Washington as president. The writer of a history of the congregation on its fiftieth anniversary noted it had served "as a counterbalance to orthodoxy, superstition and bondage of any kind." It was a good way to sum up the work and purpose of a most unorthodox church.

Frontier Justice in Perry County

I

t was a scandal most dreaded, in a community founded on the strongest of Christian principles. A spiritual leader was accused of sexual immorality, misusing funds, teaching false doctrine, and ignoring fellow leaders. And this was not any leader.

Martin Stephan brought about 750 traditionalist Lutherans out of Saxony in 1838 to a promised land in America. The group's vision helped found the basis of the conservative St. Louis–based Lutheran Church–Missouri Synod. But that was ahead.

Their voyage grew out of restriction of religious expression, fear of incarceration, and unhappiness over the rationalistic theology promoted by the Saxon State Church. By the late 1830s, the community talked of coming to America. Members read Gottfried Duden's tales about a paradise in Missouri and decided to settle there. Stephan and his group arrived in several ships in New Orleans in January 1839. They made Stephan bishop before they docked and came to St. Louis. They caused a stir, including in the antireligious St. Louis German-language newspaper the *Anzeiger des Westens*.

Part of the group, including Stephan, relocated 110 miles downriver from St. Louis to Perry County, Missouri. There, their enthusiasm for Stephan turned cold. People contended Stephan was dictatorial, lavished luxuries on himself, and misused the colony's funds. Then several women confessed that they had had sexual relations with Stephan. One was Louise Guenther, who had treated him for eczema in Germany. C. F. W. Walther, a pastor who had stayed in St. Louis with other colony members, was given the task of seeking Stephan's removal from office.

On May 30, 1839, an eleven-member council of pastors that included Walther approved his excommunication and removal from office. The same day, Stephan was told he had to leave his home and community immediately. He refused but relented when a mob that had been waiting outside burst in. Stephan was given one hundred dollars, clothing, and a few belongings. The rest of his property, including land and a library with fifteen hundred books, was taken from him. That night he was made to sleep in a tent. The next day Stephan—sixty-two and in ill health—was taken at gunpoint across the Mississippi and abandoned. Guenther followed him to Illinois. It "was hard to prove that responsible parties had instigated the riot, though that was certainly the case," the prominent German attorney Gustave Koerner wrote after representing Stephan in suits to regain his property in 1842. Koerner wrote that his client won settlements consisting of a small amount of cash, some land, and personal property that had been badly damaged by flooding. In 1845, Stephan became pastor of Trinity Lutheran Church in Red Bud, Illinois, and was buried with honor in the church cemetery after he died in 1846. To the end, he denied the charges against him.

Walther took a different path. In 1839, members of the Saxon community who remained in St. Louis named him pastor of Trinity

Martin Stephan

Lutheran Church–Missouri Synod

Lutheran Church to succeed his brother, O. H. Walther, after his death. Saxons were sent to pastor churches, and Walther started promoting a Saxon view of Lutheranism in a paper called *Der Lutheraner*. From 1847 to 1850, he served as the first president of the new German Evangelical Lutheran Synod of Missouri, Ohio and Other States, which later became The Lutheran Church–Missouri Synod. He served again in that post from 1864 to 1878 and died in 1887. Today, the synod honors Walther as its founding father and often takes little note of Stephan.

One descendant of Stephan did take note. In *In Pursuit of Religious Freedom: Bishop Martin Stephan's Journey*, Philip G. Stephan laid out a list of injustices he contended leaders of Martin Stephan's community did against his ancestor. They include expelling him without a trial, making public confessions of adultery that were meant to stay confidential, and the crimes of theft and kidnapping. Walter Forster's generally anti-Stephan book about the Saxon migration to Missouri, *Zion on the Mississippi*, offers the view that Stephan was given one hundred dollars and a few belongings as a quick and dirty way to settle claims of malfeasance against him. Fiehler Gerard has a different take on the argument. Gerard is a staff member at the Lutheran Heritage Center and Museum in Altenburg, Missouri, which includes exhibits on Stephan's Perry County settlement. Pioneer circumstances in Perry County in 1839 were different, a local judge told Gerard. People didn't go through channels when they discovered a horse thief, he said. "A horse thief would have been hung the next morning." Perhaps the best way to describe the voyage of the Saxon Lutherans to Missouri is that it started with a passion for religious freedom and ended with frontier justice.

Mayor William Dee Becker, left, boarding
glider with community leaders, August 1, 1943

The Mayors

St. Louis German-American Mayors

he Germans with the biggest influence in St. Louis often were the ones who moved into the mayor's office. The city's eight German-American mayors remade the downtown map, began the project that led to the building of the Gateway Arch, and adorned the city's highways and byways with perennials.

First among the German mayors was Henry Overstolz, who was born in Prussia, a direct descendant of the oldest patrician family in Cologne. He became mayor in 1876 after the St. Louis City Council tossed out results of a tainted election that showed an opponent had won. He was mayor during the disastrous 1876 split with St. Louis County that locked in the city's boundaries forever. When voters tossed him out in 1881, the *St. Louis Post-Dispatch* headlined, "The Defeat of Kaiser Overstolz Assured."

Henry Ziegenhein served from 1897 to 1901, while St. Louis was recovering from the Great Cyclone of 1896. Once he called four children who were caught stealing dogs into his office for a lecture on clean living. "You must obey your mothers after this and keep away from other people's henhouses and dog kennels," he admonished them before letting them go.

Under Frederick Kreismann, who served from 1909 to 1913, the city started regulating food, and the Municipal Courts and Central Library buildings downtown went up. But a free bridge across the Mississippi went unfinished because a $3.5 million bond issue wasn't enough to finish the job.

Henry Kiel, mayor from 1913 to 1925, presided over the passage of $87 million in bond issues for improvements ranging from fixing the River des Peres to the auditorium and opera house that bore his name.

Bernard F. Dickmann was mayor from 1933 to 1941, when the Jefferson National Expansion Memorial was established. While the Old Cathedral and Old Courthouse were saved, forty blocks containing some of the city's oldest buildings were bulldozed.

After he was elected mayor in 1941, William Dee Becker fought boss rule, pushed to end public gambling, and sought a new airport, possibly near the confluence of the Mississippi and Missouri rivers. But he'll always be known best for being one of ten civic leaders killed in a tragic crash of a military glider before ten thousand people at Lambert-St. Louis Municipal Airport on August 1, 1943.

An FBI agent before he entered politics, John Poelker narrowly defeated Mayor Alfonso J. Cervantes for the city's top spot. Then he served during the construction of the Cervantes Convention Center, renamed America's Center. When Poelker died in 1990, the legendary South Side Alderman Albert "Red" Villa said Poelker had enough German in him that he wouldn't take any nonsense from anybody.

While he served from 1981 to 1993, Vincent C. Schoemehl Jr. worked for downtown revival, promoted public-private partnerships, and was known for the slogan, "Ready Fire Aim," for his leadership style. He led an effort to plant millions of daffodils around St. Louis.

German–American Mayors

Eight St. Louis mayors claim German heritage

From Munster to City Hall

When Henry Overstolz lost the election for mayor twice in one year, it seemed public life was behind him, but the German immigrant wasn't about to give up. Overstolz lost the mayoral race in 1875 but ran again a few months later after the man who had defeated him died. Overstolz lost that election as well. However, the election was a fraud, he charged, and demanded a recount of the results. In February 1876, after a recount, the Board of Aldermen ruled that Overstolz had won the election, and St. Louis got its first German-born mayor.

Overstolz was proud to say he was a direct descendant of the oldest patrician family in Cologne. He was born in Munster, Westphalia, Prussia, on July 4, 1822, and came with his parents to America in 1836. They settled across the river from St. Louis in St. Clair County, Illinois. He moved to St. Louis in 1846 and opened a general store the next year. He was elected to the Board of Aldermen in 1849, sold his store in 1851, and spent the next sixteen years running sawmills. From then on, he rose in the business and political life of St. Louis. In 1853, he was elected the city's first German comptroller. He kept the job for two terms but was defeated by a Know-Nothing Party candidate when he ran for a third term. He was elected to the Board of Public Works in 1856 and served as City Council president from 1871 to 1873. Then he set his eyes on the city's top job.

It seemed Overstolz was destined to live out his life in the private sector when he lost to Arthur Barret in April 1875. But Barret died a few months later, and a special election was set to name a replacement. Overstolz ran again, this time against James H. Britton. When votes were counted, Britton was declared the victor, but stories of foul play circulated. Some said wagons full of inmates showed up at polling places to vote for Britton. Late on February 9, 1876, the City Council ruled, sixteen to ten, that Overstolz had won by 138 votes. The next morning, Britton ordered police into City Hall and refused to leave his office. But Overstolz took over when the Missouri Supreme Court ruled in his favor.

Overstolz was mayor in August 1876 when residents of St. Louis City and County voted on a plan to enlarge St. Louis City and break it off from the county. Results showed the scheme won narrowly in the city but lost overwhelmingly in the county. Backers sensed fraud, and a commission named to investigate agreed. Election officials said they had destroyed hundreds of ballots and were sworn to phony returns. Revised county results revealed that the election passed, much to the regret of city leaders ever since.

Overstolz won re-election in 1877 and soon found himself in the midst of a nightmare. In July, workers in St. Louis joined with one million strikers throughout the nation. Already angry over wage cuts brought on by the Panic of 1873, they were outraged when railroads slashed pay even more and crushed protests by their workers. On July 22, railroad and bridge company workers stopped freight traffic in East

Henry
Overstolz

Mayor, 1876-1881

St. Louis and peacefully took over the city's depot, yards, and street. The following day, they took control of the St. Louis Union Depot and its yards, and five thousand protesters gathered at the Lucas Market. Soon, strikers were in charge of the city, but then police and civilian militiamen accompanied by the mayor marched out and ended the strike without bloodshed.

It was a high point of the administration of a mayor who found himself out of favor with city residents who thought he was in the hands of machine politicians. He ran for another term in 1881 but lost by a heavy margin to William L. Ewing. "The Defeat of Kaiser Overstolz Assured," the *St. Louis Post-Dispatch* headlined, when it was clear the mayor had lost.

After his terms as mayor, Overstolz served as president of the city's Fifth National Bank, which he organized in 1860 as the Tenth Ward Savings Bank. On November 7, 1887, as he lay dying of heart disease, the bank failed. For years, he said its assets were sound, but its books were a mess. Its cashier was arrested for making false entries. Overstolz was not aware the bank was closed when he died on November 29, 1887. A grand jury didn't find enough evidence to prosecute him, but questions remained whether Overstolz should have known about the reckless condition of the bank's books. So it was that the life of this pioneering German politician ended in a shadow.

A German Builder
Rebuilds St. Louis

ost St. Louisans would guess that the grand old auditorium at Fourteenth and Market streets had something to do with somebody named Kiel. They'd be correct. Long before the edifice reopened in 2011 as the Peabody Opera House after a $78.7 million restoration, it was called the Kiel Opera House. Mayor Henry Kiel fought to have a place fit for the finest entertainers and speakers in the land, but his real achievement was the promotion of a major package of bond issues in 1923.

Kiel was born in St. Louis in 1871, the son of Henry and Minnie Kiel, who had immigrated to the United States from Hanover, Germany. The son of a bricklayer, he learned his father's craft before entering the construction business. Over the years, he helped erect such buildings as Soldan and McKinley high schools, the Coronado Hotel, and the current Post-Dispatch building.

Politics, however, pulled Kiel from the construction trade. "A man shouldn't depend on politics for a living," he said in 1909. "But if he wants to go into it for fun, there's plenty of fun in it." A Republican, he lost his bid for sheriff in 1912 and narrowly won the race for mayor the next year. Quickly, he pushed for a bond issue to finish a free bridge across the Mississippi. Construction had started under a $3.5 million bond issue but stopped when the city ran out of money. He was less successful promoting a $10 million Central Parkway between Market and Chestnut streets. City residents who thought it would be a speedway for the rich voted it down. The mayor thought it was a lost opportunity but consoled himself with the passage of a new city charter in 1914 that doubled his salary from $5,000 to $10,000.

After his re-election in 1917, he did his part to open the Municipal Opera—now the Muny. He was on the wrong side of public opinion when he favored franchise concessions and a tax drop for a streetcar

Henry Kiel

Mayor, 1913-1925

company. He also successfully fought for the Forest Park location for the city zoo. There also were those who thought his German heritage made him less than a patriotic American during World War I. A committee that formed to meet former President Theodore Roosevelt on a stop during a speaking tour decided Kiel shouldn't introduce him. Roosevelt saw Kiel as a patriotic American and asked him to make the introduction.

All of this would have made for a memorable time before Kiel left office in 1925. But what set Kiel apart from other mayors was his backing of $87 million worth of bond issues in 1923. In today's dollars, the bonds backed by a wide group of civic and business groups called for spending well over a billion dollars worth of improvements. Kiel and other civic leaders launched a major campaign that included a reel that played in city nickelodeons and movie houses. Only a $1 million National Guard armory failed to get the two-thirds majority needed for passage.

The package of improvements included fixing the flood-prone River des Peres, hospitals, firehouses, power plants, waterworks improvements, parks, playgrounds, streetlights, and widened streets. Downtown, the bond issues paid for a new Civil Courts Building, the Aloe Plaza, and the municipal auditorium and opera house that bore Kiel's name after he died in 1942. People today are still benefiting from the effects of that gift to the future. It was a major legacy for a son of a German bricklayer.

Barney Dickmann
Goes to the Mat

e can't help you, the attorney general said. Don't even bother the president. Go away. A lot of other mayors who heard that would have gone away and told the newshawks waiting for a story, "Well, we tried." But Bernard F. Dickmann, a German-American who was mayor of St. Louis from 1933 to 1941, gave the president an offer he couldn't refuse. The president backed down, and the St. Louis riverfront never was the same.

Dickmann—most called him Barney—learned the ways of politics early. His father, Joseph F. Dickmann, was born in Prussia in 1856, immigrated to the United States, settled in St. Louis, and married Maria Eilers. Born in 1888, Barney Dickmann, one of six children, grew up while his father was elected mayor three different times. He went into real estate and climbed the Democratic Party ladder. In 1933, he was swept into the mayor's office on the same Democratic wave that made Franklin Delano Roosevelt president the year before.

The new mayor went to bed as late as 1:30 a.m., but he was always up by 5:45 a.m. so he could ride his black horse "Big Boy" in Forest Park before work. Then he rode off to City Hall, where he worked like a horse to get what he wanted for St. Louis. With his prodding, a $16 million bond issue was passed to finish projects not yet completed from earlier bond issues and put the jobless to work. Soon, he was working on an even bigger project, which would change the way the whole world views St. Louis. He made the acquaintance of Luther Ely Smith, a lawyer and citizen activist who proposed clearing a moribund warehouse district on the riverfront and replacing it with a park around a memorial just as imposing as the Washington Monument. Soon, Dickmann was pushing for local and federal money for the monument, to be called the Jefferson National Expansion Memorial.

That done, Dickmann and Raymond Tucker, commissioner of the city agency that dealt with smoke pollution, turned to passing a tough ordinance to clear up the city's smog. Though the law eliminated smoke so thick motorists sometimes turned on their lights at midday, Dickmann was convinced the law was a major factor in his defeat for a third term in 1941. But two years later, he started a new career when he was appointed city postmaster—a job from which he retired in 1958.

It made for a glowing resume but didn't tell the rest of the story. In 1968, after the Gateway Arch had been erected, Dickmann revealed how some behind-the-scenes arm-twisting kept Luther Ely Smith's dream alive. It was late in 1935, and St. Louisans were looking for federal money to start clearing land for the riverfront memorial. Planners predicted the project eventually would cost $30 million. Actually, Congress had approved an outlay, but the president still had to sign an executive order for the money to be released. Attorney General Homer Cummings nixed the idea. He told the president that he couldn't approve an order that depended on future federal funding.

Dickmann turned up the heat. "I told him: 'Mr. Attorney General, you can be sure that St. Louisans—and Missourians, aren't going to take this lying down,'" Dickmann told a reporter for the *Globe-Democrat* in 1968. "I reminded him that Mr. Roosevelt would be up for re-election shortly,' I said—and he knew I wasn't kidding," Dickmann said. "'You can be certain that he won't carry Missouri if he doesn't give us the green light on the riverfront—now. I'll see to it that he doesn't, if I have to campaign against him personally.'"

Cummings apologized, but stated there was nothing he could do. The next day, as *Globe-Democrat* staff writer Walter E. Orthwein told the story, Cummings called Dickmann: "'I've got good news for you—good news. We've just found a new law that will enable the president to go ahead and sign the riverfront order.'" That law allowed the Department of the Interior to receive title to historic sites as national shrines. The federal government came through with $6.75 million to match the city's $2.25 million. And Dickmann was convinced it wouldn't have happened if he hadn't dug in his heels.

A Tragedy at Lambert

Had anybody asked Mayor William Dee Becker how he wanted to be remembered, he might have said he kept his word to fight boss rule in St. Louis. But then nobody asked him that question before he boarded a military glider with nine others the afternoon of Sunday, August 1, 1943, at what was then called Lambert-St. Louis Municipal Airport. Becker rode with the crew of Captain Milton C. Klugh and glider mechanic Private J. M. Davis. With them was the demonstration's sponsor, William B. Robinson, president of Robertson Aircraft Co., which made the glider. Others who piled in included St. Louis Chamber of Commerce President Thomas Dysart and Henry L. Mueller, who as presiding judge of the St. Louis County Court was the county's chief executive. Also along for a romp in the sky were city Public Utilities Director Max Doyne, Deputy City Comptroller Charles L. Cunningham, Robertson Aircraft Vice President Harold A. Krueger, and Lieutenant Colonel Paul H. Hazelton of the U.S. Army Air Force. Ten thousand people—including Becker's wife—watched in anticipation as a plane towed the craft two thousand feet into the air and released it. They gasped when the right wing buckled and broke off, and the plane went into a nosedive. The craft landed with a thud and exploded. A crash siren sounded. Dozens of women fainted. Others wept.

Becker's tragic death at age sixty-six contrasted with the way he had climbed to the post of mayor. He was born in East St. Louis in 1876, the son of Germans who came to the United States when they were young. His father, John Philip Becker, started life in Germany, moved to Paris, and found himself in St. Louis at seventeen. He worked as an accountant and lived at a boarding house with another German, future Anheuser-Busch beer baron Adolphus Busch. Family lore had it that Busch offered John Becker a part in a brewing venture. Instead, he opened a store, first in East St. Louis and then in St. Louis. William Becker's mother, Anna Cammann, was born in Bremen, Germany, a daughter of a Lutheran minister who fled Germany after the 1848 rebellion failed.

William Dee Becker grew up in the posh Lafayette Park neighborhood and graduated from Harvard. He studied at the St. Louis Law School, the predecessor of the Washington University Law School. He became a probate lawyer, married, moved in high society circles, and had two children. In 1916, he was elected to a twelve-year term as judge of the St. Louis Court of Appeals, which served Eastern Missouri. He was re-elected in 1928 but lost a bid for a third term in 1940.

Becker turned his attention to defeating Democratic Mayor Bernard Dickmann. The Republican hammered Dickmann for machine politics and won. Once in office, he instituted a new merit system, opposed job buying, and abolished the post of city lobbyist in Jefferson City. He demanded that city police end public gambling and curb vice. A pilot, he led a successful $4.5 million bond issue campaign to expand Lambert-St. Louis Field. He promoted a new airport, possibly near the confluence of the Mississippi and Missouri rivers.

With his enthusiasm for flight, it is not surprising that Becker used gallows humor during a news conference the day before the glider flight. "Gentlemen, you can die only once, and we all must die some time," he joked. He praised Board of Aldermen President A. P. Kaufmann, who would become mayor if Becker died. "If anything should happen to me, I'm leaving an able man to step into my shoes." By the end of the next day, Kaufmann was mayor. Checks determined that the wing fell off because of a defective part in a wing-strut fitting that inspectors missed. Missouri Senator Harry Truman, who was leading hearings on waste, corruption, and inefficiency, spoke of the crash in part of a radio address he dropped because of time constraints. "Had we checked earlier and criticized the company for installing these defective parts, the president of the glider company, like United States Steel and Curtiss-Wright officials, might have resented it. But the mayor would be alive today."

At City Hall, a plaque went up honoring those who died in the crash. It includes: "*Dulce et decorum est pro patria mori*," a line from *Odes*, by the Roman lyrical poet Horace. The words mean, "It is sweet and fitting to die for one's country." From the East Coast, the *New York Sun* wasn't criticizing Becker for getting on the glider, but it gently suggested that "the proper place for him or any other officer of large responsibilities is a place involving a reasonable minimum of personal risk." It was one instance when it was best to pass on an invitation.

The City's Brightside

hen Vincent C. Schoemehl was mayor, reporters took note of a sign in his office with a decidedly German message. The plaque put up by the last mayor of German descent read, "Ready, Fire, Aim." Some would say it was an admission he was prone to act first and think later, but Schoemehl contends the impression was out of context. The advice actually comes from the management consultant book *In Search of Excellence: Lessons from America's Best-Run Companies*, by Thomas J. Peters and Robert H. Waterman. Schoemehl said the real meaning is that it's better to act than to wait for every scrap of information. "It's a phrase that I still think is very pertinent to the way you do business," Schoemehl said.

The slogan seems appropriate for a descendent of Germans, who are known for bold, quick action. Actually, Schoemehl is only a quarter German. He is half Irish and a quarter Polish, but he is proud of his German heritage.

Schoemehl traces the German branch of his family to Frederick (Fritz) Schoenmehl, who was born in the village of Gundheim, about thirty-five miles southwest of Frankfurt, Germany. Early in 1866, when he was twenty-four, he boarded the ship *America* at Bremen, Germany. He arrived in the United States around April, just two months before Prussia and Italy began their Seven Weeks War with Austria and several German states. A family legend has it that Fritz high-tailed it out of Germany so he wouldn't have to fight in the war.

Fritz settled in the Soulard neighborhood of St. Louis and married another German, Elizabeth Otto, in 1873. They moved in with Elizabeth's father, Nicholas Otto. Fritz worked as a painter and bartender before he died in 1910. In his death certificate, his name is spelled "Schoemehl," without the "n" before the "m" he had when he arrived in America.

Fritz's son Henry sold jewelry and shoes. During the Depression, he sold magazines door-to-door. Henry's son Vincent Sr. was a housepainter and wallpaper hanger. Vincent Sr. married Lucille (Wojciechowski) Miller. They had eleven children, all of whom still live in St. Louis. Vincent Jr. was born in 1946. He grew up in Pine Lawn, graduated from the old DeAndreas High School, and moved to the city's Skinker DeBaliviere neighborhood in 1965. After receiving his history degree from the University of Missouri–St. Louis, he sold office equipment and started an advertising and marketing company. Then he began his political career.

"I just got to know some of the neighbors," Schoemehl said. "It was the 1968 presidential election. We were all opposed to the Vietnam war," he said. So he started working as a volunteer for Eugene McCarthy's presidential campaign. It was the kind of thing his great-grandfather Fritz might have done. In 1975, at twenty-eight, he was elected alderman in the Central West End's Twenty-Eighth Ward. Only six years later, at thirty-four, he defeated incumbent James Conway to become mayor. While he and his wife, Lois (Brockmeier) Schoemehl, sent their two children to St. Roch's School in the West End, he stayed in office for three four-year terms. He chose not to run for a fourth term in 1993, the year after he lost a bid for the Democratic nomination for governor.

Like most politicians, Schoemehl saw a mix of good and bad results

Vincent C. Schoemehl

Mayor, 1981-1993

while in office. The football Cardinals left town, and Schoemehl couldn't find the money needed to follow through with a pledge to reopen the shuttered Homer G. Phillips Hospital on the North Side. Population decreased and crime went up, but that wasn't his fault. He claims one accomplishment was bringing down pension costs, including those for police officers and firefighters. In his first term, the number of city employees dropped from about 11,350 to about 4,700. Downtown saw steady growth, and his Operation Brightside initiative helped with neighborhood cleanup, recycling, and painting over graffiti. Operation Brightside is best known for the planting of perennials ranging from tulips to crocuses to the favorite daffodils. Now called Brightside, the organization celebrated its thirtieth anniversary in 2012. "Operation Brightside was, I think, a major success. People still talk about it, and they pop up every spring," Schoemehl said, referring to the bulbs planted.

Schoemehl remained active after he left office at the relatively young age of forty-six. Until 2001, he had an alternative energy consulting business. Since then, he has been president and CEO of Grand Center, which promotes and works to revitalize the arts district around North Grand Boulevard generally between Lindell and Delmar. He suspects his German lineage didn't hurt him as he climbed the ladder to the city's highest position. "It was helpful in my political career because at the time there was a very strong German heritage," Schoemehl said. "Certainly the German name helped."

German Cultural Society

Recent Years
1946–present

GERMAN CULTURAL
SOCIETY
← PARKING

After 162 Years, Still Going for the Carom

nce, craftsmen pushed elephant's tusks into lathes and turned them while they used a cutting instrument to form ivory into useful shapes. Pipe bowls. Silverware handles. Bracelets. Billiard balls. Skilled ivory turners did well. Ernst Schmidt did very well with the trade after he left Celle, Germany, and arrived in St. Louis in the mid-nineteenth century. He set up shop downtown in 1850 and started selling ivory billiard balls, ten-pin balls, and smoking pipes. Pool balls pushed everything else out, so he made that a specialty.

A.E. Schmidt Billiard Co. is still around. In its sixth generation, the family business is one of a handful of American companies that still make pool tables. It no longer makes ivory balls. It stopped importing ivory in 1966 when it became illegal. The company kept making balls from ivory imported before 1966 until around 2005. "It's not something that we'd really want to do," said company owner Kurt Schmidt, Ernst's great-great-grandson. "Not only is it politically correct, but it's a waste." Today's super-hard plastic balls are as good at making bank shots as any ivory ball—and they are better for elephants.

In Ernst's day, his ivory balls did so well that he branched into billiard tables. He found markets for them in pool halls and in breweries seeking to entice saloons to switch to their products by giving away pool tables. Ernst followed a notably German business style. "He was very frugal. Didn't spend much money on anything," Kurt said. "He wanted his family with him. And really not much has changed. We've all been about the same way."

The company grew after Ernst's son Oscar joined the firm. Oscar eventually named it A.E. Schmidt Co. for his wife, Anna Elizabeth

Schmidt. His sons, Edwin and Ernest, were challenged when Prohibition closed bars and the Depression killed business. Ernst's philosophy of frugality was passed down to his son and grandsons, which helped them get through the Depression. Since they couldn't afford a truck, they delivered tables—piece-by-piece—in streetcars. They offered credit when others didn't. In good times, they reasoned, people would remember that. The firm expanded and started shipping tables throughout the country.

A new generation arrived when Edwin's two sons, Arthur and Harold, joined the company after World War II. They promoted their product in two TV programs in the 1960s, "Beat the Champ" and "Billiards for Dollars." The later went national for a couple of years. Arthur's son Kurt was eighteen when he started with the firm. He has always loved it, he said. Under Kurt, the factory moved in 2004 to 720 Koeln Avenue in South St. Louis. It has a local store in West St. Louis County. While tables haven't changed, technology has made it easier to make them. In three minutes, computerized routers add details like fleur de lis that once took craftsmen days to complete. At the firm's plant, completed wooden parts are lined up awaiting assembly on a floor with a light covering of sawdust. In another room, pool table rails with a fresh coat of finish dry on a rack.

The company makes about one thousand tables a year, but the Chinese are bearing down. The firm is one of only four surviving American pool table makers. Nonetheless, Kurt remains hopeful. So does his son Michael, who's joined the business. Kurt doesn't think the Chinese can match the quality. It may be the German in him. Germans are stubborn, he said. He is proud of his heritage. And, in case you are wondering, Kurt does play pool but says he's not good at it.

Germans from Eastern Europe

ohn Pappert is one of those Germans who took a roundabout way to make it to America. Today, as the president of St. Louis's German Cultural Society, he looks back at how he got here. Founded by displaced Germans like himself, the society is dedicated to the heritage of all Germans. The route that Pappert's ancestors took to come to St. Louis began in Southwestern Germany in the eighteenth century, when the empire of Austria-Hungary issued a call: Come to our land. Their population had been decimated when German-Austrian forces defeated the Ottoman Empire in their area.

People moved to Eastern Europe—to places like Romania, Hungary, and Serbia—and were called Danube Swabians. "They were primarily farmers and craftsmen," Pappert said. He might still be living there today if it wasn't for World War II. Pappert, who was born in a village near the city of Timisoara, Romania, in 1937, saw his father drafted into the German army and killed on the Russian front in 1943. A year later, the Russians marched into Romania, and Pappert's family was on the run.

"We left by wagon train and fled ahead of the Russian front," Pappert said. For six years, Pappert's family was in Austria as displaced people. But in 1950, they moved to St. Louis, where they had relatives who had immigrated here around 1900. Pappert became an engineer, got married, and had three boys. In turn, they presented him with four grandchildren. Pappert dedicated himself to the German Cultural Society, which traced itself to the St. Louis Chapter of the American Aid Association. Founded in 1945 to help German refugees from Germany and Eastern Europe, it turned toward preserving German heritage after the refugee crisis ended. In 1969, it adopted its current name.

Today, the German Cultural Society has about 450 members, a building and hall at 3652 South Jefferson Avenue in St. Louis, and the

Donau-Park in House Springs, Missouri. The younger generation that comes to events like the annual Oktoberfest in September may not remember everything that went before, but the older group is trying to keep the memory alive. The newsletter on its website has an ad for Amerika Woche, a St. Louis German Rock Band. It has a trivia column in German and brief items about the *Natur-und Wandergruppe*, the *Seniorengruppe*, the *Festkomitee*, and the *Gartenverein*.

The group's leaders know that the way for the society to survive is to reach out to the younger generation. Herbert and Monika Lorenz are doing just that by involving their two sons, who are in middle school and high school. "I've been active in that group since I was a little girl. I'm first-generation American," said Monika, a chemist who lives in South St. Louis County. Her mother is Danube Swabian and her father was from the Black Forest in Baden-Württemberg of Southwestern Germany. "They met in St. Louis and got involved in the German Cultural Society," she said.

Herbert is an ethnic German who came to America from Romania in 1990, after the fall of communism. He is in the moving business and met Monika at the St. Louis Strassenfest. To ensure their children knew their heritage, they sent them to a weekend school run by the German School Association of Greater St. Louis. Every two or three years, the children go to Germany to see Herbert's parents. In that way, the Lorenzes are keeping the link strong. "There's a lot of culture there," Monika said. "We want to keep those traditions going for our kids."

"It's Getting
Less and Less"

arvey Ries is old enough to remember a different time. He was milking cows when he was six and learned his three "R's" in a one-room school in rural Illinois. He didn't know a word of English until he started attending that school. Ries spent his first years learning German with members of his extended family and with neighbor kids. His generation, which grew up in the 1930s, may have been the last in heavily German Monroe County that grew up learning the language of the Fatherland in the home. "If I see somebody who knows German, he and I or she and I will speak a few words," Ries said. "It's getting less and less."

At eighty-two, Ries is still active enough to climb a ladder next to a cherry tree beside his house between Columbia and Waterloo, Illinois, and prune little branches with a snipper and big ones with a small power saw. Most of his career, Ries worked for the Missouri Pacific Railroad and lived next to a farm that members of his family still work. He doesn't know when his ancestors came from Germany, but he does know he is related to Jacob Maeys, the founder of the German village of Maeystown in southwestern Monroe County.

Germans started immigrating to the United States in the 1830s. When Maeys founded his village in 1852, Germans were pouring into Monroe County and changing its character. "The German language predominated in many parts of the county, and in the stores, the shops, and even in the courthouse *wird deutsch gesprochen*," said *Arrowheads to Aerojets*, a history of Monroe County published by the Monroe County Historical Society in 1967. "Many of the remainders of the old American stock understood the German perfectly and spoke it fluently," the book said. "The German schoolmaster and, above all, the German priest or clergyman, by their ceaseless efforts succeeded in perpetuating the language of the Vaterland on the banks of the Mississippi River."

By the time Ries was born, the tongue was already dying off in Monroe County, and everywhere else for that matter. The parents of his wife, Marion, knew German but made it a point that she didn't learn it. "They wanted to be able to talk about something and the children wouldn't hear it," he said. But Ries's parents kept up the tradition and shared it with their children, even though they knew English. "When I was three years old, my dad had a hired hand who spoke no German." When he started going to the Mueller School on Steppig Road in Monroe County, older students translated what the teacher was saying. "The teacher didn't know any German," Ries said. But Ries did just fine. "They didn't spend millions of dollars to try to teach the foreigners English," Ries said. "By the time I got out of first grade, I could speak English."

Ries married Marion in 1951. They had five children, ten grandchildren, and four great-grandchildren. His daughter, Diana Hamilton, recalls that Ries would talk in German with his father. When Ries and his wife visited Germany in the 1980s, he used a German slang expression he'd learned that meant "The people were talking." The Germans' response: "We haven't said that in years." In fact, the expression had left popular use in Germany more than one hundred years ago. The expression dated back to the early 1800s, when Ries's ancestors brought it to the United States. Ries kept speaking German with his old friends, even after his wife's death in 2009. "It's getting less and less," he said. "We're all dying off."

Columbia and Waterloo

Harvey Ries

The Eleven-Year Vacation

Bill and Fred Stock were two American kids on an adventure after their parents took them on an extended vacation to Germany in May 1939. Everything was fine, their parents William and Maria Stock reasoned. Hitler had made peace with his neighbors. The boys could see the land their parents left to come to America in 1926. They would be back at their home at 7105 Page Avenue in St. Louis in October. But on September 1, 1939, Germany invaded Poland, and the Stock family was stuck in Germany for the remainder of the war.

"My mom was pregnant, and we registered with the American consul in Berlin to return to the United States," said Bill, who lives in the Compton Heights neighborhood of St. Louis. "Then my dad told the German authorities that we're going to leave and go back to the United States." It didn't matter that his parents were naturalized American citizens. You were born in Germany, live in Germany, and are eligible for the draft, they told William. Your wife and children can go. Maria, who was pregnant, reasoned she might not be able to make a living in America. So she and the children stayed.

As Bill Stock recounted the story, he sat with his wife, Maritza, one Saturday afternoon at a table of the bar of the family's restaurant, the St. Louis Gast Haus at 1740 Chouteau Avenue in St. Louis. He opened the German restaurant in 2003 with his wife, her sister Ann Sueme, their daughter Carmen, and her son Edward. In another room, diners later would feast on sauerbraten and schnitzel near a floor-to-ceiling mural—full of deep blues, oranges, yellows, and greens—of Berlin's Brandenburg Gate.

Bill knows well what happened around that gate as the war began. "You're stuck there, and you go along with the flow," said Bill, a retired meat cutter. The family lived in an apartment complex with about fifty other foreign families that were in Germany when the war began. Their father found work as a welder and never was drafted. The boys were nine and eleven in 1939 and did what boys that age did anywhere. They went to school, played soccer, and made friends.

Hitler's influence was everywhere, but the boys tried to live a normal life. "We were kids. We didn't pay any attention to propaganda," said Fred, of South St. Louis County. "In school, there was not really a lot of talk about the war," he said. The family lived in Brandenburg an der Havel, about sixty miles west of Berlin. It was close enough for both to go into Berlin on a train. "We saw Hitler in parades in Berlin," said Fred, a retired lithographer and father of one. Bill and three other friends tried unsuccessfully to sneak into a stadium where Hitler appeared at a soccer match. A sympathetic guard let them in. They saw Hitler speaking at the other end of the stadium, behind about 100,000 fans.

Bill estimates eighty to ninety air raids were close enough to hear. A bomb once fell about twenty yards away. Worse were the rationing and hunger at the war's end. His mother started the war at about 140 pounds and ended at less than 100 pounds.

On May 1, 1945, the Soviets burst into town. "It was total chaos and fear not knowing what to expect," Bill said. On June 15, the Soviets put the family on a westbound train. That began two and a half months of staying in camps and crisscrossing Germany in trains. The Stock family wound up at the home of their paternal grandfather in Schwabach, Germany. Bill and Fred found work as interpreters for American military police and returned to St. Louis in 1950. Their parents lost their citizenship because they were out of the country. Bill and Fred's brother John, who was born in Germany, never was a U.S. citizen. The three made it to America in 1955 as immigrants. Bill was drafted in 1951 and went to Korea. In 1955, he married Maritza Fingerhut, an ethnic German who had lived in Serbia. She and other family members became refugees when Soviets invaded their land in 1944. They came to America in 1950.

Fred believes his wartime experiences made him more giving. Seeing all the misery and dead people made him want to help others. Now he provides food and supplies for food pantries. Bill believes they made him want to look at how people in other countries see things. "I'm American leaning because I'm an American first, but I'm an internationalist," he said.

Still Turning

Several times a week, Romy and Rose Hetz head down to the Concordia Turners at 6432 Gravois Avenue to bounce on a trampoline, tumble on a mat, and otherwise have fun getting fit. When they are at the Turners, the two preteens are following in the footsteps of their father, Concordia Turners President Ross Hetz, and three generations before him who joined the group. They are part of a 137-year-old organization founded to help German immigrants develop sound minds and bodies. Concordia was one of a number of St. Louis turnvereins—from the German *turnen*, meaning "to practice gymnastics," and *verein*, meaning "club, union." In some ways, they performed the same purpose as the modern YMCA. The difference, though, was that this was a place for Germans to gather, exercise, and prepare for the next Napoleon.

The turvereins began with the German patriot Friedrich Ludwig Jahn. Known by Germans as the *Turnvater*, or Father of Gymnastics, he was born in Lanz, Germany, in 1778, studied theology, history, and literature from 1796 to 1802, and then became a tutor. It was a time of turmoil, not one that encouraged the scholarly life. Napoleon was conquering Europe. When his armies decimated the Prussians at Jena and Auerstaedt on October 14, 1806, it meant the end of independence for much of Germany.

Jahn joined the Prussian army and hatched a plan to help bring freedom back to his land. He would use gymnastics to build men strong enough to defeat the occupiers. He moved to Berlin in 1809 to become a teacher and to develop an outdoor program of gymnastics. Deciding there was a better way to get fit, he invented such exercise equipment as the horizontal bars. His movement spread like wildfire after he opened his first *Turnplatz*—open-air gymnasium—in 1811. Motivated by his writings, young men who trained in the gymnasiums saw themselves as the front line in the battle against Napoleon. After liberation came in 1813, the *Turnverein* movement spread throughout Germany. Many who

Concordia Turners

Ross Hetz, president, Concordia
Gymnastic Society, with daughter Romy

exercised in the gyms were at the center of the German revolts of 1848.
When Germans came to America, they brought the movement with
them. In 1848, they founded the American Turners in Cincinnati.

The Turners caught on among St. Louis's German immigrants. The
first of them, the St. Louis Turners, started in 1850 and had more than
five hundred members when the Civil War began. Its members made up
four companies in the Union Army. Members of other turnvereins did
the same. They were among thousands who volunteered to fight for the
Union after the surrender of Fort Sumter. They called on their training
when they surrounded the Confederate-leaning state militia camp at
Camp Jackson on May 10, 1861, ending any serious threat that Missouri
would leave the Union. After the war, the St. Louis Turners and similar
groups prospered. By the end of the nineteenth century, the St. Louis
Turners had about seven hundred members. Theirs was one of many
Turner organizations where Germans came together for exercise and
fellowship. Such was the feeling about the Turners and its founder that
the North American Gymnastic Union (*Nord Americanischen Turnerbund*)
dedicated a monument and bust to Jahn in Forest Park in 1913.

Over time, though, turnvereins disappeared. The St. Louis Turners
merged with the South Side Turners in 1918 and closed in 1940. The
story repeated itself throughout the area. Today, the Concordia Turners

is the only Turner organization in St. Louis with a building. Founded in 1875, it was in a hall at Thirteenth and Arsenal streets from 1877 until the early 1960s. When planners decided to build the new Interstate 55 in the path of the hall, the organization sold it to the state in 1962 and moved to the present location the next year.

Today, about eighty-five families and twenty-five individuals belong to the Concordia Turners. When it's open, members perform gymnastics, aerobic exercises, karate, swimming, and a host of other activities. More than one hundred years ago the Concordia Turners sent teams to competitions in Germany, as well as to the 1904 Olympic Games in St. Louis. They continue to send athletes to events like the National Festival of the American Turners every four years. The group isn't just for Germans. Neighbors often join for the convenience. But at the core are families that remain generation after generation. At the onsite bar, such longtime members talk about old times. Charles Wietrop, forty-eight, the group's secretary, said he is the third generation of his family to be in the Concordia Turners. He is not sure how long the organization can hang on. "The prognosis? It's always been iffy," he said. But, he added, it's been on the edge of extinction for forty years.

Too Much of a
Good Thing

ile this in the "It seemed a good idea at the time" basket. Actually, it was a great idea, but not for the little town of Columbia, Illinois. In 1961, the year after census takers counted 3,174 souls in their town, members of Columbia's Chamber of Commerce were looking for a way to bring more people to their upcoming sidewalk sale. Remembering Columbia's rich heritage, they gave it the German name *Strassenfest* (Street Fair) and prepared for the crowds on Main Street. Then they prepared for people to drive from South County across the Jefferson Barracks Bridge.

Coins rolled in for the downtown stores and groups like the Holy Name Society and Khoury League, so the Chamber of Commerce made it an annual event. Soon everybody heard about it. Effervescent local TV personality Charlotte Peters did her part by promoting it endlessly on her show. Large groups of Columbia's townspeople in German outfits showed up for programs where she told one and all to come on out. In early years, when seven thousand to twelve thousand people showed up for the whole weekend, townspeople reveled in the attention, while local groups counted the cash they took in selling brats and beer. But by the end of the decade, people stopped smiling. The town's police estimated the crowd at the 1971 Strassenfest at 35,000 to 40,000. Others put it as high as 100,000.

The crowds and cars overwhelmed the little town. The oceans of brew sold by vendors made some revelers too boisterous for Columbia's police to handle. Townspeople shielded their kids' eyes when some of the out-of-towners passed up Porta Potties to relieve themselves on lawns. The traffic snarl became impossible when everyone left at the end of the night. When police made sixty-seven arrests at the 1971

Strassenfest, the City Council decided it had had enough and called off any future celebration in Columbia.

After 1971, the Strassenfest continued, first in downtown St. Louis, then in the Westport Plaza shopping center of West St. Louis County, and finally in Chesterfield. Crowds in the hundreds of thousands turned out for the celebration of German heritage. The group holding the Strassenfest called a pause to the event in 2011 and 2012 but promised it would be back. For many in the St. Louis area, the memory of a night spent at the Strassenfest brings joyous thoughts of all things *gemütlichkeit*. In Columbia, it brings thoughts of mixed blessings.

German Funeral Homes

Barry Schrader wouldn't have it. No daughter of his would work on bodies in his funeral home, or any woman, either. Ruth Schrader Arft still went into the room where they embalmed the bodies at the family's funeral home on Manchester Road in Ballwin. "I saw the bodies on the tables, but I never was permitted to watch the process," she said. When she was old enough, she helped arrange funerals and did business but never worked on bodies. Today, at ninety, she's the matriarch of Schrader Funeral Homes and Crematory, a 144-year-old West County business.

Founded by Arft's great-grandfather, the company is part of a proud tradition of St. Louis funeral homes founded by Germans. One of the earliest was founded by Christian Hoffmeister, an immigrant from Hanover, Germany, just before the Civil War. Hoffmeister arrived in St. Louis in 1844 and opened the Great Western Livery Stable in 1858 in what is now the 7800 block of South Broadway. He founded a horse-drawn public carriage line and then provided horses and carriages for funerals. The company soon was in the funeral business. Dignity Memorial, a national chain of funeral homes, acquired Hoffmeister in 1991. That was nearly a decade after Dignity Memorial acquired Kriegshauser, another local funeral home founded by a German, in 1982. George Kriegshauser started the business in 1891.

John L. Ziegenhein & Sons Funeral Home is a local funeral home founded by a German-American that remains independent. In 1900, John L. Ziegenhein Sr. and his four brothers founded the funeral home at the corner of Texas Avenue and Cherokee Street on the South Side. They had help in a high place: their uncle, St. Louis Mayor Henry Ziegenhein. In 1931, John L. Ziegenhein Sr. opened his own funeral home at 7027 Gravois Avenue. In 1995, the company he founded

An early
Schrader hearse

opened a second location at 4830 Lemay Ferry Road. When no immediate family members were available to take over the business, it passed
into the hands of key members of the extended family in 1995.

The St. Louis Public Library's online listing of funeral homes,
parlors, chapels, and undertakers since 1886 includes a number of
homes with decidedly German names. Biederweiden had one location
in the North Side, and another on Chippewa Street near Grand, not far
from the Wingbermuehle Funeral Home. North St. Louisans attended

the Bromschwig and Heitzenroeder homes, while the Oxenhander home offered funerals at 4460 Washington Avenue.

Schrader Funeral Homes and Crematory has withstood the test of time as well as the pressures to sell out. The business began in 1868 when Frederick Schrader started making coffins for his neighbors in a building just east of the firm's current home at 14960 Manchester Road. Schrader came to the Ballwin area in 1846 and started making furniture. It was natural that he would add coffins as a sideline. Soon, Schrader and his son, William, were also providing carriages and horse-drawn hearses for funerals, while keeping the furniture store. Seeing the importance of the business, William went to school to learn embalming and received his state embalmer's license. The family built a new funeral home, second-floor dwelling, and furniture store in 1910. With additions, that building is at the core of the present Schrader building.

Ruth Arft remembers growing up in that building, the daughter of William Schrader's son Harry F. Schrader and his wife, Ethel. For this youngster, there was nothing unusual about growing up among the dead. "People used to say, 'Aren't you afraid?'" she said. "It was such a part of my life that I never considered it." Arft held on to that attitude after she married Henry "Hank" Arft, who played first base for the St. Louis Browns from 1948 to 1952 and then followed his wife into the family funeral business. After Harry retired in the 1960s, Ruth and her brother Harold A. "Skip" Schrader became co-owners and funeral directors. Hank was active until he died in 2002. Harold is semi-retired and Ruth retired, but both still are involved in the business.

Today, a fifth generation handles the operation: Peggy Arft-Goethe and her husband, Dennis Goethe, and Steven Schrader and his wife, Cathy. In recent years, the firm bought another funeral home at 108 North Central Avenue in Eureka. Nathan Arft, the son of Peggy and Dennis, has indicated he wants to join the family funeral business before his parents retire. This funeral home is one German-American business that refuses to die.

The Man Who
Wouldn't Stop

I t was 9:20 on the morning after Thanksgiving 2011. Ed Golterman should have been happy. Less than two months before, the Kiel Opera House had reopened as the Peabody Opera House, after Golterman had spent thirteen years badgering, cajoling, campaigning, and generally making life miserable for anyone who didn't share his enthusiasm for opening the place again. But on this morning, he was on the phone to Charlie Brennan's fill-ins on KMOX to gripe—pleasantly, but still to gripe. Something wasn't quite right, he told John Hancock and Mike Kelley. Why was the place dark on Thanksgiving weekend of all times? He was gentle and positive about it, without anger or rancor. Still, it was clear staying shut on a holiday weekend was not what Golterman had in mind.

It sounds like typical German stubbornness, only more so. But Golterman is only a quarter German. "I'm half Italian, so that gives you some of the passion," he said. The final quarter is Irish. The real stubborn German was his grandfather, Guy Golterman. An attorney and special investigating counsel, Guy Golterman went after corruption in the City Health Department. But his real love was the opera.

On the wall of Ed Golterman's apartment in Kirkwood are pictures of Guy Golterman and some of the performances he promoted. Ed keeps a framed carbon copy of a letter Mayor Henry Kiel sent to Guy after the opening of the Municipal Opera in Forest Park. Both had worked hard to get the place opened in time for six showings of the opera *Aida* during the thirteenth annual convention of the Ad Clubs of the World. In the letter, Kiel spoke of a bond issue "which will provide a liberal appropriation for a municipal auditorium which it seems . . . could be built in such a way as to supply the requirements of an opera house at least for the present."

Six years later, a package of $87 million in bonds approved in 1923 provided money for construction of the auditorium and opera house that was named for Kiel after he died in 1942. Kiel's construction company built the opera house. Before the building opened in 1934, Guy traveled to Europe to study opera houses and sign singers and conductors. The opera company for the new hall included a singing chorus of one hundred and a dancing chorus of thirty. Over the years, Harry Truman, Bob Dylan, Frank Sinatra, and the Grateful Dead performed at the Kiel Opera House. In 1990, the St. Louis Board of Aldermen proposed to tear down the Kiel Auditorium on the opposite side of the opera house and build what is now the Scottrade Center. The next year, the Kiel Opera House closed.

For seven years, the opera house was empty. Then Ed Golterman decided he couldn't stay on the sidelines. Golterman, the son of an administrative assistant to four St. Louis mayors, threw himself into the effort to reopen Kiel. He had been a television broadcaster and produced industrial training and marketing films and videos for twenty-five years. But, he said, "I couldn't keep doing that and save the opera house." So he quit and outlined a $48 million plan to renovate, reopen, and market the place. Then he refused to go away. To him, it was what downtown needed to compete with other cities. "I went through everything. I went through my savings. I went through my retirement." When he had to work, he worked as a security guard. "I heard every insult and every lie," he said. Then came a financing package to renovate the opera house into a performing arts and cultural center. Golterman exulted when the doors reopened. He thinks Guy did too. "I think he's very proud. I think he assigned me to do this," he said.

Guy Golterman

An Operatic Legacy

Friedrich Jahn Memorial, Forest Park

Places

The Vacation That Started a City

A doctor-prescribed steamboat trip along the Rhine River led to the founding of the industrial town of Granite City, Illinois. Granite City is a short jaunt from downtown St. Louis. Niedringhaus Avenue—the town's main street— goes past other streets at a forty-five-degree angle. It passes factories, the Granite City Cinema, City Hall, the old YMCA building, and the Gateway Regional Medical Center.

The story of how Niedringhaus Avenue came to be in that spot began in Westphalia, Germany, in the early 1850s, when Frederick and Mary Niedringhaus left Germany and came to America. One of their children, Frederick G., opened a tin shop near the St. Louis riverfront in 1857. Five years later, Frederick G.'s brother William became his partner. Weary of cutting up tin and soldering it together, they imported a machine from France that quickly stamped knives, forks, and spoons from one sheet of tin. Demand became so heavy that Frederick G. and William Niedringhaus incorporated the St. Louis Stamping Co. in 1866. But success proved too much for William. Exhausted, he consulted a doctor who ordered him to take time off and forget the business.

Obeying his physician, William headed to Europe, where he took a trip down the Rhine. On a stopover in a small village, he found pots and pans covered with a smooth white enamel. William's vacation was over. He saw the potential of this product and had to have it for the family business back home. William took his luggage from the steamboat and paid five thousand dollars for the right to spend weeks learning the technique. Back in St. Louis, he worked with his brother to use ground granite to make what they would call graniteware. After they made their first piece of graniteware in 1874, they were granted a patent. For three years, they imported their iron from Wales. Then the mill in Wales burned. Their answer was to build the Granite Iron Rolling Mills in St. Louis to provide their own sheet iron.

In 1888, Frederick G. was elected to Congress and stayed on for just one term. He wasn't just in Washington to help the people. He supported legislation that would provide protective tariffs for the tin industry. Soon after the legislation passed, the Granite Iron Rolling Mills started producing another product, tin plate. Frederick G. didn't run for another term and soon found himself with a serious problem. The business boomed, so much so that the brothers needed more room. They considered building a bigger plant in North St. Louis but decided they couldn't get the rail connections they needed. The owners of property next to their existing plant wanted too much money. Then a solution came, in a new connection to Illinois.

Plans were underway for a new Merchants Bridge across the Mississippi River north of St. Louis. William and his son George Niedringhaus found a spot north of where the bridge would come into Illinois. It was a small and attractive community around a rail stop called Kinder. Soon, the Niedringhaus family got options on thirty-five hundred acres. While some in the family wanted to name the place Niedringhaus, Granite City won out, in homage to their product. The founders laid out their city according to a plan developed by the St. Louis city engineer that was similar to Washington, D.C.'s. This plan called for Niedringhaus Avenue to extend diagonally through the street grid, as Pennsylvania Avenue does in Washington. They planted fourteen thousand trees and incorporated the town in 1896.

One of the first plants the family laid out was Granite City Steel, to provide material for the graniteware. It is now the U.S. Steel Granite City Works. Other plants that followed included the Granite City Stamping Co., which was renamed the National Enameling and Stamping Co. (NESCO) in 1899. Seeing the benefits of diversification, they brought other plants to town. Welshmen, Armenians, and immigrants from Central Europe came to work in the factories. The graniteware made in Granite City was known everywhere and stayed strong until after

World War II. By 1956, though, competition from aluminum pots and pans, stainless steel, Pyrex, and Corning Ware forced NESCO to shut down. But the industrial town of Granite City remained. It's home to nearly thirty thousand people, down from a high of more than forty thousand in 1970. The city today might not exist, if not for William Niedringhaus's inspirational trip down the Rhine.

Granite City

Frederick and Mary Niedringhaus

German Names in South County

An item in the *Missouri Republican* on December 13, 1875, offered evidence of the influence Germans have had in South St. Louis County. The article told of a meeting held the previous Thursday to name a growing community on Lemay Ferry Road four miles south of St. Louis. Those who came to the powwow at J. G. Baker's store elected as their chairman Charles Mehl, a German who was awarded a land grant in South County in 1846 for fighting in the country's war with Mexico. Even then, his family had been established in the area. So it came to the surprise of no one at the meeting that Mehlville was one of four possibilities—and the eventual winner—offered as a name for the growing community. The happy inhabitants of the newly named hamlet adjourned to eat, hoist toasts, and hear a speech in German by John Wagner. Then Mehl closed the evening by thanking everyone for naming their town after him, its oldest resident.

Not many students at Mehlville High School may know the story, nor the taxpayers of the Mehlville School District, nor those who depend on fire protection or ambulance service from the Mehlville Fire Protection District. But the German-derived name of Mehlville is one example of the many ways the German farmers who poured into the area in the nineteenth century influenced the development of South County. For example, Oakville, that area south of Interstate I-255 and east of Interstate 55, doesn't seem to be German. But it received its name from a man with a German moniker, J. S. Schulte. The justice of the peace for the area, Schulte considered all the oak trees that hugged its roads and named it Oakville.

Another of those German residents was Johann Georg Aff, who came to America in 1858. After staying in Pennsylvania, he moved to St. Louis and farmed on rented land close to the present location of

Forman and Weber roads. Aff married a fellow German, Maria Loesch, in 1860 and farmed until 1867. He spent the next three years in St. Louis and then acquired land at Tesson Ferry and Gravois Road. He opened a country store and saloon, and the spot became known as the Ten Mile House because the St. Louis Courthouse was ten miles east on Gravois. Aff became a U.S. citizen in 1873, and three years later, he received his postmaster's commission and called his new post office Affton. When the area incorporated in 1931, the new municipality took the name. But this was the Depression, and people who wondered where they would find their next meal didn't care much about having their own city hall. Hard-pressed to find the money to run their town, residents voted to dissolve the city in 1935. But in 1931, the local school board voted to change the name of District No. 47, McKenzie, to the School District of Affton.

Johann Georg Aff had done well in using his naming rights. When people in St. Louis think of the place around Gravois Road west of St. Louis, they think of the community Johann Georg Aff named. So do the customers of Affton Heating and Cooling, the Affton Veterinary Clinic, and Affton Trucking. So it was that Germans throughout South County left an imprint that remains today.

A Sinking Boat and an Alligator

The earliest groups of Germans to come to what would become Washington, Missouri, arrived because of the sinking of a vessel in the Mississippi River at St. Louis. Had the boat not gone down in 1833, members of twelve German-Catholic families from Belm and Osterkappeln, near Osnabrueck, Germany, would have boarded the ship for a voyage up the Illinois River. As it was, the immigrants found another boat, but not one headed for their chosen destination. It was going up the Missouri River. They considered their plans carefully and followed the second boat to a different destination. The call of Gottfried Duden, who had spent time on the Missouri River in the 1820s and wrote glowingly of the land around the river as a promised land, rang loudly in their minds. They wanted to settle on the north side of the river at a new town called Marthasville, but the captain cautioned that the north side of the Missouri wasn't a healthy place. He counseled that they settle on the south side, around where a man named William G. Owens had formed a settlement.

In October 1833, they landed at Owens's settlement, which was little more than a handful of houses by the Missouri River. The group started a German-Catholic church, now called St. Francis Borgia Parish. They spent the first winter in several quickly erected huts and the smokehouse of Bernard Fricke, a German who had arrived in the area with his family a year earlier. Other groups followed. Seven families from Hanover arrived in 1837. Even more followed. By the end of the 1830s, the land was laid out as Washington. They made their living as wool carders, blacksmiths, tile makers, weavers, stone masons, and farmers. One of them, John B. Busch, founded a brewery in Washington in the 1850s. It

was several years before his younger brother Adolphus Busch went into the brewing business with his father-in-law Eberhard Anheuser.

In time, the Germans settlers in Washington banded together to strengthen the mind and body. On December 13, 1859, they founded the Washington Turnverein, a local version of the gymnastics societies that filled Germany and anywhere German immigrants settled. Without a building, they exercised in a meadow, in a market hall, and an upper room of the city hall. The turners held picnics, marched in parades, danced at balls, and spent time in target practice. But the Civil War brought a change. Members signed up for Company G, 17th Missouri Infantry, the Turner Brigade. They were known as skilled riflemen. Turnverein meetings were suspended on July 6, 1862, and came back to life after war's end. Its members built a hall at Third and Jefferson streets in 1866 and found abundant opportunities for dances, feasts, dramas, and drinking.

Franz Schwarzer joined the Washington Turnvereins at the end of the Civil War. He and his wife immigrated to the United States in 1864.

Heeding the words of Duden, they came to Warren County, where he became a gentleman farmer. He flopped and moved to Washington the next year. Soon he set up shop in the zither business. He had experience in Germany making a stringed instrument, which is halfway between a small harp and a guitar. Zithers were no ordinary musical instruments. Neither were the mandolins and guitars he made. Schwarzer won a gold medal for his products at the International Exhibition at Vienna in 1873 for showing "significant progress in new inventions (and) in the introduction of new materials and contrivances." The most famous zither maker of the last half of the nineteenth century, he sent his instruments throughout Europe and to places such as Peru and Chile.

Back home, Schwarzer loved exploring caves with his friends. He bought a city block in Washington for his house, factory, and the greenhouse where he kept his tropical plants in the winter. It was a favorite place for bands to play and musical groups dedicated to the fine art of zither playing. When visitors got bored, they could admire Schwarzer's pet alligator as it roamed the property.

Franz Schwarzer

Washington, Missouri, zithers

A German Outpost on the North Side

rederick Kraft didn't have to think hard about a name for a new community north of St. Louis. He was born in Baden-Baden, Germany, immigrated to the United States, and settled around the main road between St. Louis and points north in 1852. Kraft started a saloon and general store at Broadway and Bittner Street called the Six Mile House, because of its distance from downtown St. Louis. According to a commonly accepted story, he submitted the name "Baden" for a new post office in 1860. He became the postmaster, and the name Baden was accepted. Other businesses grew around the Six Mile House in this German outpost.

Baden was a fitting name for the new community. Many of the Germans who came to the area in the 1840s and 1850s settled there. It was so popular that people took to calling it "Germantown." A new subdivision in 1856 got the name "Railroad Addition to Germantown." That same year, the year of the first St. Louis Fair, Kraft and Jacob Bittner started a line of horse-drawn carriages to carry passengers down Broadway to East Grand. A German-American named Walter Espenschied built a market house in 1862 at what is now 8200 North Broadway. Two large cemeteries in the area—the nonsectarian Bellefontaine and the Catholic Calvary—were far from being German, but Friedens United Church of Christ Cemetery at 8915 North Broadway is unquestionably German in origin. It was started in 1862 by what was then called Friedens German Evangelical Church near what is now the corner of North Broadway and Riverview Drive.

Germans were an important part of Holy Cross Catholic Church. Before it was built, German Catholics who lived in the area had gone to Mass at a chapel of the Carmelite Convent in Calvary Cemetery. But in 1863, Kraft sold a group of Catholics two acres for a church. Dedicated in 1864, the church had seventeen Irish families, fifteen German families,

Baden

Holy Cross Catholic Church

and three French families the next year. But the influence of Germans was clear from the beginning. The church's founder, the Reverend Caspar Doebbener, was born in Germany, as was every pastor until 1976. It soon was obvious that there was an uneasy peace between Germans and Irish at Holy Cross. The Irish dominance of the American Catholic Church made matters worse, as did different languages and cultures. In 1872, eighty Irish families pulled out of Holy Cross and founded their own church, Our Lady of Mount Carmel. Nearly broke, Holy Cross—now made up largely of poor German laborers—hobbled on. One of its pastors, the Reverend Peter Wigger, exemplified the spirit of the church when he said, "Succeeding generations shall know who built this church. We did not solicit or beg from anyone outside our own parish. We are too proud. We are no beggars. We are Germans." Germans played a major part in the church for decades. In 1940, the parish still had enough Germans to allow an occasional German Mass.

As Holy Cross struggled with the loss of its Irish parishioners, Baden dealt with the loss of its separate identity. Baden was part of the area St. Louis swallowed up when it expanded in 1876. At the time, the town had four hundred inhabitants, eleven stores, three wagon shops, and four churches. It had a public school, two Catholic schools, and a Lutheran school. The strong German influence continued for a while, but other groups also moved in, including African-Americans. The community remained. The Kraft House at 1086 Bittner Street stands as a reminder of the early resident who gave the community its name, but many of the other parts of the old German community are gone.

A City of Statues

o Henry Shaw, William Shakespeare was the perfect choice for a statue in the middle of Tower Grove Park. But Shaw, the founder of the Missouri Botanical Garden and donor of the land for Tower Grove Park, did not turn to an American to fashion his statue. He contracted Ferdinand von Miller of Munich, Germany, to mold his monument to this greatest of writers. The statue, formally unveiled on April 23, 1878—Shakespeare's birthday—faces east, with one foot slightly advanced and his right hand holding a quill pen. Another von Miller creation—a statue of the German naturalist and explorer Alexander von Humboldt—rests at the Grand Boulevard entrance to the park. In his best finery, von Humboldt gazes into the distance, frowning. The two works of art are among the statues and monuments in St. Louis with German themes or creators.

Memorial Plaza, at Market and Fourteenth streets in Downtown St. Louis, holds a bronze monument for the historian and poet Friedrich von Schiller. It is based on a sculpture by Ernest Rau in von Schiller's birthplace of Marbach, Germany. The German-American businessman Harry J. Kiener paid for the Kiener Memorial Fountain and Runner Statue in Kiener Plaza downtown. He ran the half-mile for the U.S. track team in the 1904 Olympics in St. Louis. Portland Place and Lake Avenue in the Central West End hosts the sculpture "Mercure s'amuse" (Mercury Teasing the Eagle of Jupiter) by Frederick Wellington Ruckstuhl. And the Lutheran Church–Missouri Synod's Concordia Seminary in Clayton has a statue of Martin Luther by Ernst Frederick August Rietschel.

One German-made statue-monument caused a scandal when it was dedicated in 1914 in Compton Hill Reservoir Park. A committee of German-Americans largely bankrolled by beer baron Adolphus

Busch intended to praise the dedication of St. Louis German-American journalists Carl Schurz, Emil Preetorius, and Carl Daenzer to the unadorned facts. So German sculptor Wilhelm Wandschneider, the winner of a competition to design the monument, did just that. His monument "Naked Truth" included a statue of a naked woman.

A less-controversial monument is at Jefferson Avenue and Arsenal Street in Benton Park. It's a memorial to Friedrich Hecker, a German revolutionary who settled on a farm near Belleville, Illinois, after the failed German revolution in 1848 and fought in the Civil War. Sculptor G. Stubenraugh created an obelisk with Hecker's name and the dates "1848" and "1861" on them.

In Forest Park, German-American sculptor Charles H. Niehaus produced a work that is recognized as a symbol of St. Louis. Across the street from the entrance to the Saint Louis Art Museum, he made a large bronze statue of the crusader King Louis IX of France, the namesake of St. Louis. In the "Apotheosis of St. Louis," the king is on his horse and holds up a sword by its blade. Both appear ready to jump off their giant-sized pedestal and dash down Art Hill. "Hercules and the Hydra," a bronze statue sculpted by Mathias Gasteiger in Germany, sits close to the "Apotheosis." Forest Park also contains the Jahn Memorial, commemorating Friedrich Ludwig Jahn, who founded the gymnastic and fraternal society, the Turnverein. And those who like statues of war heroes should love the one in Forest Park of the German-American Civil War General Franz Sigel, also by sculptor Robert Cauer.

There is an excellent military statue in Lyon Park at Broadway and Arsenal Street, complete with the obligatory soldier on a horse. It memorializes the capture of the Missouri militia encampment at Camp Jackson on May 10, 1861. That action by Captain, and later General, Nathaniel Lyon and the Missouri Volunteers—largely made up of Germans—ended any serious anti-Union threat against St. Louis.

A Taste of the Fatherland on St. Louis's Streets

he only real way to cure homesick Germans is to return them to the Fatherland. But if they only want a taste of home, they only have to drive through St. Louis. Street names they encounter will remind them of the people, places, and things they would see every day in Munich, Saxony, or Berlin. True, no signs bear the name of the German capital. "Patriots" saw to that during the anti-German hysteria of World War I when they changed the name of the Central West End's Berlin Avenue to Pershing Avenue in honor of General John J. Pershing. But Germania and Allemania streets survived (*Allemania* is the Latin and Spanish word for Germany).

Homesick Germans can find avenues named after the cities of Bremen, Cologne, Dresden, Salzburg, or Hildesheim. Beethoven Avenue honors the famous composer, while Goethe Avenue is named for the German poet, dramatist, and novelist Johann Wolfgang von Goethe. Schiller Avenue is named for the German philosopher, poet, historian, and dramatist Friedrich von Schiller. German words also are noted on street signs. Kettler Road comes from a German word for "one who mended pots and kettles, a tinker." And the basis of Dischinger Court is "disch" for cabinetmaker.

Germans away from home may find solace in the names of St. Louis streets, but German-American natives of the city may find reason for pride in those names. More than twenty streets names are for Germans who helped build St. Louis. Sigel Avenue honors Civil War Union General Franz Sigel, who fought in Missouri and at the Second Battle of Bull Run. Steins Street is for Jacob Steins, who helped bring many Germans to Carondelet. Geyer Avenue honors Henry Geyer, a

pro-slavery German senator from Missouri who argued against Dred
Scott before the U.S. Supreme Court. Koeln Street in the Carondelet
neighborhood is named for an early merchant in the area, Christian
Koeln. Eichelberger Street is named for George F. Eichelberger,
who was on the first city council in the community of Carondelet.
Landowner Susan R. Etzel is the namesake of Etzel Avenue in North
St. Louis. The signs were another indication of the influence Germans
had in the city's development. They showed how many individual
Germans influenced their adopted town so greatly that someone
wanted to name a street after them.

Eichelberger Avenue
Berthold Avenue
Baden Avenue

Anheuser-Busch

Beer, Brats, and Baseball

When Beer Was King

f you had one hundred German settlers, the saying went, you had a brewery. St. Louis in the middle of the nineteenth century had many more than one hundred Germans, and many more than one brewery. From the 1840s to Prohibition, Germans dominated brewing in St. Louis. In the 1860s, Germans ran 80 to 90 percent of the city's breweries.

The German influence in St. Louis brewing began in 1809, when a newspaper ad announced that barley and hops were available at John Coons Brewery. Local historians say there is a good chance brewers operated earlier in the village, but Coons' ad in the *Missouri Gazette* was the earliest solid evidence of a brewery in St. Louis. Coons likely was a German. Then in 1810, Jacques St. Vrain partnered with the German brewmaster Victor Habb to produce ale, porter, and "common" beer at a brewery on Bellefontaine Road. Brewers who followed during the next two decades were of various nationalities. It wasn't until around 1840 that other German breweries started in St. Louis. Then—like the German population in the city—the number of German breweries in St. Louis exploded.

One German brewer, Johann Adam Lemp, pioneered the use of lager beer, a clear and brilliant product that could be stored longer than ale. Lemp quickly took over the local market. After he found caves in South St. Louis capable of keeping the lager cool, he built a brewery over them near present-day South Broadway and Cherokee Street. Other brewers rushed to store beer in South Side caves.

While some brewers were known for innovation, John Gaul was noted for his wife's odd habit. While Gaul was establishing his Atlantic Brewery at Park Avenue and Thirteenth Street in the early 1860s, people said his wife was busy stealing clothes. She blamed neighborhood ruffians until police searched Gaul's house. They found clothes of all sorts, enough to start a clothing store.

In 1857, the *Missouri Republican* remembered with sadness a time some decades prior when there were no Germans and therefore no beer gardens. "(W)hen they did come in it was tempestuously; a sudden and almost unexpected wave of emigration swept over us, and we found the town inundated with breweries, beer houses, sausage-shops, Apollo Gardens, Sunday concerts, Swiss cheese and Holland herrings. We found it almost necessary to learn the German language before we could ride in an omnibus or buy a pair of breeches, and absolutely necessary to drink beer at a Sunday concert." The article said beer had been "well-nigh universally adopted by the English-speaking population, and the spacious beer halls and extensive gardens nightly show that the Americans are as fond of the Gambrinian liquid as those who had introduced it."

Entering the competition to provide that Gambrinian liquid were the combination of Germans Eberhardt Anheuser and his son-in-law Adolphus Busch. In the Bavarian Brewery and then E. Anheuser Co.'s Brewing Association, they took an increasing chunk of beer sales. With the introduction of Budweiser and a name change to Anheuser-Busch Brewing Association, the company was destined to dominate the local brewing industry.

Brewers in the 1880s—whether they were Anheuser-Busch or just serving a few taverns—found themselves under attack by British conglomerates. They aimed to cash in on the profitable St. Louis beer trade by buying breweries for their St. Louis Brewing Association. Numerous German brewers sold out to that association and then brought their customers to new breweries they formed soon afterwards. The Brits never made the killing they had anticipated.

German brewers outwitted the St. Louis Brewing Association but encountered a bigger opponent in Prohibition. The push to outlaw alcohol was brought on in part by a sincere desire to stop excesses. But nativism and anti-German sentiment during World War I also was a factor. Before Prohibition, there were nearly twenty St. Louis brewers. About a third as many started up afterwards.

Of Ghosts and
Brewmeisters

I t could be a cloudy white silhouette of a man walking, slouched, with his hands in his pockets. The bulge in his belly hints that he may have consumed more strudel and beer in his day than proper. The silhouette hides part of a painting and a plush old couch in the background. The entry with the picture in the secondhand-souls-4occult.com website noted it was taken during a visit to the Lemp Mansion on DeMenil Place in South St. Louis.

Those who put the website together are hardly alone in their interest in the mansion. Built as the home of the Lemp brewing family, today it serves as the thriving Lemp Mansion and Restaurant. Much of its success as an eatery and bed and breakfast is due to the stories of ghosts at the house and four sensational suicides by Lemp family members. While fascinating, the tales overshadow the important role the old German family had in the city's brewing industry from the middle of the nineteenth century to the start of the twenty-first.

The Lemp family's St. Louis story began in 1793, when Johann Adam Lemp was born in Eschwege, Germany. He worked as a master brewer, immigrated to America in 1836, and came to St. Louis in 1838. He opened a grocery store and soon used his skill as a brewer to slake local thirsts. Around 1840, he became one of the first brewers in the country to produce lager beer. In porters and ales, yeast rose to the top. But yeast in lagers stayed at the bottom of the brewing kettle and produced a taste that caught on quickly. Two dozen breweries in St. Louis produced 60,000 barrels of lager beer in 1854. Six years later, 40 made 189,400 barrels. And Lemp was out in front.

Brewing lagers required a cool place to store the beer while it aged. Lemp found the refrigeration in a limestone cave under what is now Cherokee Street and DeMenil Place. He cooled it with winter ice from the Mississippi River and filled the cave with his beer. After Lemp died

in 1862, his son William took over and moved the brewery to the area of the caves where he stored his beer. Production skyrocketed, and only the upstart Anheuser-Busch came close. By the mid-1880s, Anheuser-Busch had passed Lemp. Nonetheless, Lemp was a national player and the first to distribute its product coast to coast.

When Lemp introduced Falstaff beer in June 1899, it seemed the twentieth century would be bright. But the new century brought nothing but tragedy. Despondent over his bad health and the deaths of a son and a close friend, William J. Lemp Sr. shot himself in 1904. In 1920, Lemp's daughter Elsa Lemp Wright killed herself. By that time, Prohibition had shut down the brewery. In 1922, the Lemps sold the fourteen-acre brewery complex at Lemp Avenue and South Broadway to International Shoe for $588,000, a pittance compared to its $7 million pre-Prohibition value. Depressed, William J. Lemp Jr. killed himself six months later. Ending the string of tragedies, another son of William Lemp Sr., Charles Lemp, killed himself in the Lemp home in 1949. The home became a boarding house and fell into disrepair before the Pointer family bought it in 1975. The family renovated it and reopened it as the Lemp Mansion and Restaurant.

Meanwhile, International Shoe used the brewery complex to make shoes until production moved overseas. After it was sold in 1992, unsuccessful efforts were made to redevelop it. Today the site is operated as the Lemp Brewery Business Park, with warehouses, offices, and artist studios. Many who drive by don't realize the collection of brick buildings and the gigantic smokestack once was home to a brewery that even overshadowed the mighty Anheuser-Busch.

The Lemp Brewery was gone, but it lived on in Falstaff. When others were sure beer was gone forever, brewer Joseph Griesedieck and his son Alvin were convinced it would return. They bought the Falstaff trademark for twenty-five thousand dollars in 1920. They were right. When Prohibition ended in 1933, Falstaff roared back. The ghosts of the Lemps again seemed to be in charge as their old product became one of the biggest beers in the St. Louis market and briefly was the third-most-popular beer in America in the 1950s.

Sales started falling in the late 1960s and plummeted in the next decades. In 2005, owner Pabst Brewing Co. of San Antonio stopped making the beer. That would have marked the end of 165 years of beers made and created by the Lemps if it hadn't been for the launching of a new Lemp Brewing Co. in 2004. Today, customers at the Lemp Mansion and Restaurant can drink their Lemp Lager and Lemp Jurassic Dark as they watch out for ghosts.

The Other
Busch Breweries

Brewing magnate Adolphus Busch knew what it was like to be in a big family. He was one of twenty-two children his father Ulrich Busch had between two wives. Their father grew rich through his lumber, wine, and brewing supplies business in Mainz, Hesse-Darmstadt, in the German Rhineland. With so many siblings, it is not surprising that Adolphus was actually one of three Busch brothers to run a brewery in St. Louis.

The first brewery operated by a Busch was founded by Adolphus's older brother George in Belleville, Illinois, in 1834. In 1848, George opened a malt house and brewery in St. Louis called both Busch's Brewery and Buena Vista Brewery. After adding a partner in 1854, he sold his share of the brewery in 1857 and the malting business in 1859. Before he sold out, George found time to teach the brewing business to his brother John Baptiste.

Born in Germany in 1832, John B. arrived in St. Louis when he was seventeen and went to work for George. After attending McKendree College in Lebanon, Illinois, and Howard College in Fayette, Missouri, he found himself living in Washington, Missouri, with yet another brother, Henry. John B. decided the German town fifty miles from St. Louis was the perfect place for a brewery. So around 1855, he opened the Washington Brewery in partnership with his brother Henry and Fred Gersie. The partnership didn't last, but the brewery did with John B. Busch in charge.

With the Busches well established in St. Louis, Adolphus arrived in St. Louis in 1857. Born in 1839, he was well funded from the estate of his father, who died five years earlier. Tales he later helped circulate made it sound like he was poor when he emigrated and worked his way up. They weren't true. He could afford to relax, and he did in his first few weeks in St. Louis. Later, he said he spent the time "hunting, loafing, getting acquainted and having a good time." With some cold ones, no doubt.

Soon it was time to get to work. Adolphus found employment as a clerk in a wholesale supply house. Then he became a partner of the wholesale commission business Wattenberg, Busch & Co. While there, Adolphus sometimes did business with John's brewery, which had an account with Wattenberg, Busch & Co. Wattenberg, Busch & Co. also bought George Busch's former malting company from Tinker Brothers and Co. in 1863.

The burgeoning business was good for Adolphus, but not as good as his romance with Lilly Anheuser, the sixteen-year-old daughter of Eberhardt Anheuser. Anheuser had grown rich making soap, but had been the creditor of a brewery that went bankrupt in 1859. So he bought out the other creditors of the business, called the Bavarian Brewery, and took it over with William D'Oench, a dealer in drugs and chemicals. While Adolphus was pursuing Lilly, his brother Ulrich fell in love with Lilly's sister Anna. So it was that Adolphus and Lilly and Ulrich and Anna were married in a double wedding ceremony on March 7, 1861. Ulrich and Anna left for Chicago where he found work in—no surprise—the brewery supply business.

Right after the wedding, Adolphus did like thousands of other Germans and enlisted for three months' service with a volunteer regiment protecting St. Louis. In 1864, he started as a part-time salesman for the Bavarian Brewery. Five years later, he sold his share in Wattenberg, Busch & Co. and used it to buy William D'Oench's portion of the Bavarian Brewery. With Adolphus in the firm, the company became Anheuser-Busch and was on the way to becoming a mighty force in the brewing industry.

That didn't prevent Adolphus from keeping contacts with John B. Busch. The only major interruption in the early years came in 1864, when Confederates raided the John B. Busch mansion for money and his brewery for beer. In later years, Adolphus and his offspring often would stop by to hunt and fish. John's brewery lasted until 1918, but the business continued during Prohibition by selling ice and non-alcoholic products of Anheuser-Busch. After Prohibition ended, the firm bottled Anheuser-Busch beer until it closed in 1954. Today, it is remembered as one of two other Busch breweries and as a reminder that Adolphus wasn't the only member of his family who came to St. Louis—a common pattern among immigrants.

The Family Tradition
That Won't Die

Of all the German names involved in the St. Louis brewing industry, one that pops up again and again is Griesedieck. The index of *St. Louis Brews: 200 Years of Brewing in St. Louis* lists eighteen different people named Griesedieck. It takes a long list to keep track of all the family members that have had their hands on various Griesedieck brewing ventures. Memorable brands that Griesediecks once brewed include Stag, Griesedieck Brothers, and Falstaff. IBC Root Beer, which is still available, started as a product of the Griesedieck family and the Independent Breweries Company in 1919, when Prohibition was inevitable. Henry A. Griesedieck, the last president of the Griesedieck Brothers Brewing Co., once said it was easier to talk about St. Louis breweries the family wasn't involved with than those it had its hands on.

The Griesedieck family's involvement in the local brewing industry has a long tradition in brewing going back to the 1700s. In 1766, Johann Griesedieck started brewing beer in Stromberg, Westphalia. In 1870, Anton Griesedieck came to the United States. He moved to St. Louis and got into the malting business. In 1878, he bought the Thamer Brewing Co. with August Koehler and Robert Miller. The business incorporated in 1880 as the Griesedieck Brewing Co. They sold it the next year and then bought another company, the Staelin (Phoenix) Brewery. That company stayed in the Griesedieck family until 1889, when it was sold to the St. Louis Brewing Association, owned by a group of British investors.

The Griesediecks broke from the association in 1891 to go into competition with the group in a family business called the National Brewing Company. The company prospered with such brews as Pilsner Export, White Seal, and even a brand called Willuhafa Beer.

Change came in 1907 when National Brewing Company joined with six other companies. The Griesediecks came out on top, with Henry Griesedieck being named corporate president. But once again they bolted to a new family outfit the company formed, the Griesedieck Brothers Brewing Co.

In 1912, a group led by Henry L. Griesedieck bought the Western Brewery in Belleville, Illinois. Its name was changed to Griesedieck-Western. Until 1907, that brewery had made a product named Kaiser. Then Germany's Kaiser Wilhelm became too unpopular, so the Western Brewery held a contest to name a new beer. George E. Wuller pocketed twenty-five dollars in gold for his winning entry, Stag Beer.

With Prohibition ahead, another family member, "Papa" Joe Griesedieck, formed the Griesedieck Beverage Company to make a near beer called Hek. After Prohibition started, he picked up a bargain. The once-mighty Lemp Brewery was selling off assets. A company "Papa" Joe and his son Alvin formed picked up the trademark for a mainstay, Falstaff, for a cool twenty-five grand. Some people thought Joe was crazy, but he and Alvin knew people soon would have enough of the great experiment. When Prohibition ended in 1933, Falstaff was ready to slake thirsts in St. Louis and throughout the country. By the end of the 1950s, the brand briefly was third in the nation.

Other Griesedieck brews also returned to popularity. Stag was the biggest seller in the St. Louis area right after Prohibition. Helped by commercials featuring the cartoon character Mr. Magoo, it remained a big seller. However, in 1954, Carling Brewery bought Griesedieck-Western Brewing Co. Today, Stag is a product of Pabst Brewing Co.

Griesedieck Brothers beer also prospered after Prohibition and hit a high in the early 1950s. It missed a chance to buy the St. Louis Cardinals before Anheuser-Busch snatched it. After that, sales declined while A-B's sales moved steadily upward. In 1957, Falstaff bought Griesedieck Brothers, stopped production of its brands, and started production at Griesedieck Brothers' modern plant. Within a decade, Falstaff's sales were declining. In 1975, businessman Paul Kalmanovitz bought the company and moved its headquarters to San Francisco. In

1976, it brought back GB Beer, but the public didn't buy it. The next year, Falstaff halted production of Griesedieck Brothers Beer. The days of Falstaff also were numbered. Sales fell until owner Pabst Brewing Co. stopped making it in 2004.

It seemed to be last call for the Griesediecks in the beer business, but they wouldn't have it. In 1987, businessman Steve DeBellis tried his hand at marketing a Griesedieck Brothers beer, but it shipwrecked in 1991 when the brewer he had hired to make the product went bankrupt. Then in 1992, Ray Griesedieck incorporated Griesedieck Brothers Brewery. The son of Henry A. Griesedieck, the last president of Griesedieck Brothers Brewery, Ray was determined to make the operation work. Today it continues with Griesedieck Bros. Premium Golden Pilsner and Griesedieck Bros. Unfiltered Bavarian Style Wheat.

Griesedieck breweries

A Bullet That Started a Career

ther St. Louis Germans remembered May 10, 1861, as the day they provided the men to take over a secessionist-leaning state militia camp outside St. Louis. Tony Faust had other reasons to revel in the memory of that day, for that was when he found his calling. As Faust watched those soldiers during the Camp Jackson Affair, a soldier stumbled and accidentally fired his gun. A bullet Faust took in his side weakened him enough that he had to end his life as a plasterer. The search for another way of life led him to open a downtown restaurant that would be known throughout the country. Faust's Restaurant would be a regular stopping place for the city's rich and famous.

The restaurant at Broadway and Elm Street was so progressive that Faust started lighting the inside of his building with electricity in 1878, eleven years before the city's streets. Also known as Tony Faust's Oyster House & Saloon, it served Faust Beer, brewed by Anheuser-Busch and named in honor of Tony Faust. When the brewery introduced its new super premium Michelob beer in 1896, Faust's was the first to serve it. Family connections helped. Besides managing the family restaurant and being vice president of the Fourth National Bank of St. Louis, Faust's son Edward was second vice president of Anheuser-Busch Brewing Co. Adolphus Busch married off his fourth daughter, Anna Louise Busch, to Eddie Faust on March 20, 1897.

Tony Faust's rise to being the city's premier restaurateur began in Prussia, where he was born in 1835. He came to the United States in 1853 and found work as an ornamental plasterer. After being shot on May 10, 1861, he started a bar at Broadway and Russell Avenue. He married Elizabeth Bischoff in 1865 and established his high-class eatery in 1868. When he died in 1906, he was at the top of the pile of the city's elite. After Faust died, the restaurant was managed by his son, Anthony

E. Faust Jr., before passing through two other owners and shutting down on June 30, 1916.

Newspaper articles that reported the closing also told of the restaurant's glory in the midst of the city's bright light district. "Travelers in far off lands when returning home would tell of the good meals and service they got there," the *Post-Dispatch* said. Set near the swank Southern Hotel and the exclusive Olympic Theater, Faust's was the place for great actors and actresses to dine after a performance. Nobody was more of a regular than Adolphus Busch. He was known for winning one hundred-dollar bets on whether he could identify any kind of wine poured into a glass. Another patron once won a bet by eating 256 oysters from the half-shell at one sitting. He finished his evening with a porterhouse steak, potatoes au gratin, and a stein of beer.

Faust sought to satisfy any request. A man named Joseph Jefferson arrived for supper one night at midnight. "Bring me quail on sauerkraut," he demanded. It wasn't on the menu, but the chefs obliged. "Magnificent," he said. Others agreed, and it soon was a favorite at Faust's. On New Year's Eve, Faust sat with his wife and family at a table in the center of the main dining room. At midnight, waiters placed bottles of wine in front of every patron, "with the compliments of Mr. Faust." The closing of Tony Faust's restaurant brought an end to all that. It was Auld Lang Syne for a St. Louis restaurant known the world over.

Jazz That's *Wunderbar*

n St. Louis, plenty of the early jazz came with a German riff. That's the view of Dennis Owsley, a local authority, collector, and broadcaster on all things jazz for more than fifty years. Owsley has produced a weekly jazz program on St. Louis Public Radio, 90.7 KWMU, since 1983 and set forth his extensive knowledge and impressions on the local jazz scene in his 2006 book, *City of Gabriels: The History of Jazz in St. Louis, 1895-1973*.

In his home in the Central West End, Owsley quoted Judge Nathan Young, the first black judge in Missouri and a man personally acquainted with early jazz musicians. "He said that the Germans were the music teachers, and if you want to understand the music of St. Louis, it's very much of a Germanic influence," Owsley expounded. Until after the start of the twentieth century, Germans taught African-Americans how to play. Scott Joplin was among the musicians influenced by the German teachers. Joplin taught himself how to play piano in the home of a white family that hired his mother. But he then learned the ways of European music from Julius Weiss, a music teacher who was born in Germany.

Nobody will hear the German "oompah" in jazz. Oompah is played in 3/4 time, while jazz is in 4/4 time. Nonetheless, Young claimed the music jazz trumpeters from St. Louis used was similar to what came out of the instruments of German brass bands that played here since the 1840s. The principal trumpet player of the St. Louis Symphony Orchestra in the 1920s and 1930s, an Italian man, changed his name to Joseph Gustat because of the prejudice toward German musicians in the symphony. He taught a number of black musicians in St. Louis, including the great Miles Davis. He insisted they use a trumpet mouthpiece that made a distinctive St. Louis trumpet sound.

The oompah band, meanwhile, had an effect on St. Louis Dixieland bands that are still heard today. Early on, the Dixieland bands followed the German brass band pattern of using a tuba in place of a string bass. Those who followed that style included Singleton Palmer, a tuba virtuoso who held court in Gaslight Square in the 1960s. People may not have seen the Deutschland in the music. They may think Germans are too staid for jazz music. But it's there, and *es ist wunderbar!*

The German influence on jazz

A Family Business
Comes Back

By the cliché view of what Germans do, John H. Bardenheier should have started a brewery when he arrived in St. Louis in 1865 from Oberlahnstein, Germany. Instead, he sold wine. From then to now, St. Louisans have thought of the fruit of the vine when they hear the name Bardenheier.

The nearly century-and-a-half story of the Bardenheiers in St. Louis started when John Bardenheier went to work for a wine distributor after he showed up in St. Louis. In 1873, he broke off on his own and founded the John Bardenheier Wine and Liquor Company. He plied his trade at 212 Market Street near the present location of the southern leg of the Gateway Arch. The company displayed its wines at state fairs, as well as one great big fair called the 1904 Louisiana Purchase Exposition. Bardenheier Co. sold throughout the Midwest and beyond, in states like Missouri, Illinois, Texas, Oklahoma, Kansas, Wisconsin, Virginia, Pennsylvania, Ohio, Michigan, Tennessee, Kentucky, and Indiana.

Bardenheier did well enough to acquire an eight-acre estate stretching from Grand Avenue to Virginia Avenue next to Osceola Street. In 1911, the St. Louis Board of Education bought it for sixty thousand dollars for the location of what would become Cleveland High School.

Alas, the arrival of Prohibition in 1920 brought a halt to the family wine business. When Prohibition ended in 1933, the company was back in business at 210 Market Street, next to its old address. Joseph A. Bardenheier Sr., son of John H. Bardenheier, soon needed more space and moved into 212 and 214 Market Street. A later move took the company to 1435 North Second Street. The company kept growing and moved into a 100,000-square-foot former streetcar barn at 1019 Skinker Boulevard in 1955. In the 1960s, the company was one of the top ten producers and sellers of wine by the case in America. The company sold about 1.2 million gallons in 1968. The product was on store shelves in much of the country.

When Rudy Vallee played at the Municipal Opera in 1971, he went looking for wine at a market near his hotel and bought a bottle of Bardenheier's. Impressed that the Gateway City had its own wine cellar, he arranged for a personal tour of the place, with samples, of course. While most of the plant Vallee saw was full of stainless steel vats, a few old wooden kegs remained. A German winemaker named Fritz—what else?—Doerflinger did his part to bring out the flavor of the wines.

Things looked good for Bardenheier, so good that a buyer came calling. In 1983, the Bardenheier family cashed out to Futura, a company that made synthetic coatings for insulating roofs and vats. Family members stayed on with the new owners, who noted its specialty in making linings for wine tanks made them a perfect fit. The new owners promised to pour more money into the company, decrease its product line, and shoot for the youth market. In one effort, the company hawked its products at the annual Strassenfest. But the changes Futura made weren't completely accepted. *Post-Dispatch* reviewer Joe Pollack included Bardenheier's products when he panned wine coolers carte blanche. By the early 1990s, the winery closed.

But the family name and tradition were not to be forgotten. In 2004, Wayne Evans and his wife, Kimberly Bardenheier-Evans, acquired the rights to the Bardenheier name. Kimberly is the great-great-granddaughter of John H. Bardenheier. They opened a small winery in Richwoods, Missouri, called Bardenheier Wine Cellars and started selling sacramental wine. They also started selling such specialties as "Rosie O'Grady," "Sunset Serenade," and "Blackberry Cabernet." Bardenheier wines are available in the St. Louis area at specialty stores, Friar Tuck, and some Shop 'n Save markets.

The Boss of All Presidents

Long before baseball club owners George Steinbrenner, Charles Finley, and Bill Veeck made a habit of outshining their teams, Chris von der Ahe set a standard for flamboyance that hasn't yet been matched. The German barkeep with the heavy Dutch accent became "Der Boss President" of an early St. Louis professional baseball team that was its league's champion from 1885 through 1888. The team was called the Browns, but they would usher in the twentieth century as the St. Louis Cardinals.

Some mocked von der Ahe's style and accent. Others remembered him with affection. Born in the Prussian farm town of Hille in 1851, he emigrated to the United States in 1867. The owner of a grocery and saloon at Grand and St. Louis avenues, near the Grand Avenue Ball Grounds, von der Ahe saw his place packed after ball games of a team called the Brown Stockings. So in 1881, he invested in the team and became its president.

The team, also called the Browns, became part of a new league called the American Association, a rival to the National League. Within a few years, von der Ahe's Browns dominated the Association. Among the Browns was first baseman–manager Charlie Comiskey, who went on to own the Chicago White Sox and to be the namesake for two of that team's ballparks. Comiskey offered these words about his boss: "He was when I played for him a money getter, and as every victory meant an increase in the receipts, he raved over a defeat as if he had lost $1,000. . . . Many a time did he tear into the dressing room after a game and swear at those players who may have made an unfortunate error. I simply requested him to leave, and he always did."

Der Boss President was not the only German in the clubhouse. In the early 1890s, the Browns had a "pretzel battery" made up of lefty pitcher Ted Breitenstein and catcher Henry (Heine) Peitz. On the last day of the 1891 season, Breitenstein pitched a no-hitter in his first game in the majors. Peitz was his catcher.

In 1888, von der Ahe arranged for an all-expenses-paid trip to New York for a trainload of fans to the world championship series against the New York Giants. He also ordered suits for his players during the same series, which the Browns lost. In 1915, Arlie Latham, a former Browns third baseman known for his pranks, wrote that von der Ahe's penchant for fining players and not following through was legendary. And he could change his view of a player quickly, as Latham wrote later:

> *A player came running in and found Chris serenely counting his coins.*
> *"Did you hear that, Chris?" yelled the player.*
> *"Chass."*
> *"Do you know what it was?"*
> *"Oh, I suppose that chackass Laydam made annder error."*
> *"No. But he just hit a home run with three on, and won the game for you."*
> *"I always said," remarked Chris that night, "dot Laydem vos the best man I effer hat in a binch."*

Von der Ahe matched his quirky ways with his players with flamboyant promotions. He fought a successful court battle against Sunday "blue laws" that forbade Sunday pro baseball, arguing that baseball games were recreation, not work. To the game on the field, he added a Wild West show with fifty Indians and forty cowboys and cowgirls. But the show wasn't enough to prevent a team rebellion against his dictatorial management style. He moved his team to the National League in 1892 after the American Association folded.

But the magic was gone. Von der Ahe's excesses caught up with him. The one that brought his end in baseball was the result of a fire that destroyed Sportsman's Park early in 1898. At the end of that year, the Mississippi Valley Trust Co. filed suit for failing to pay bonds taken out to rebuild the park. Von der Ahe lost the suit, and the team was auctioned off to pay the debt. The team was renamed the Perfectos in 1899 and the Cardinals in 1900. In 1902, the new American League came to town with a team called the Browns.

Von der Ahe returned to the life of a saloonkeeper, filed for bankruptcy in 1908, and often told his stories. In April 1908, the Cardinals and Browns played a benefit game for von der Ahe and gave him five thousand dollars, a goodly sum then. After he died of dropsy and cirrhosis of the liver in 1913, fans big and small mourned their Boss President. "His good nature got him a host of friends and his eccentricities lost him all his money," Latham wrote. "He was a good old fellow, when all is said, and he treated his players like men. And even if they did poke fun at him, they liked him jus' the same."

Chris von der Ahe

Owner, St. Louis Cardinals

Gussie Hits a Homer

all it a white lie. On February 20, 1953, reporters, photographers, and cameramen for the new medium of television news gathered at a news conference for an announcement. Faced with fifteen months in prison for tax evasion, St. Louis Cardinals owner Fred Saigh was selling the team to Anheuser-Busch for $3.75 million. Saigh turned down more generous offers from prospective buyers from Houston and Milwaukee after the Griesedieck Brothers Brewery of St. Louis declined Saigh's offer to sell the team to them.

Anheuser-Busch President August A. (Gussie) Busch Jr. downplayed suggestions that the brewery bought the team for commercial gain. "I am going at this from the sports angle and not as a sales weapon for Budweiser Beer," the civic-minded beer baron said. No, he said, he didn't mind that rival Griesedieck Brothers had a contract to sponsor broadcasts of Cardinals games that year.

It was all PR talk. In fact, it was one of the smartest business moves ever for Busch, the grandson of Adolphus Busch, the German co-founder of Anheuser-Busch. After Anheuser-Busch bought the team, it paid Bill Veeck, owner of the American League St. Louis Browns, $1.1 million for Sportman's Park, where both teams played. With the Cardinals securely in St. Louis, the fate of the hapless Browns was sealed. They ended the 1953 season with a last-place 54–100 record. Veeck's dream of having the Browns become St. Louis's baseball team ended. He sold the team to Baltimore businessmen who moved the team there for the 1954 season and changed its name to the Orioles. So if Gussie Busch saved the Redbirds for St. Louis, he indirectly lost the city the Browns.

Gussie looked over Sportsman's Park and decided it was a mess. He ordered a major rehab and announced he would name the place Budweiser Stadium. Baseball Commissioner Ford Frick wouldn't have it. Gussie backed down in favor of another name, Busch Stadium. He said what changed his mind was a remark somebody made about how silly it would be for the Wrigley family to change the name of its Chicago stadium to Juicy Fruit Stadium or Doublemint Stadium. No matter. In 1955 Anheuser-Busch came out with Busch Bavarian Beer, with a name mysteriously like the stadium.

Frick was happy with new owner Anheuser-Busch, but the brewery had its detractors. Colorado Senator Edwin Johnson claimed A-B bought the team to evade taxes and introduced a bill to halt the sale. Then news came out that D'Arcy Advertising Co., which represented the brewery, had decided to expand Cardinals broadcasts into Denver. Johnson was president of the minor-league Denver Bears as well as the treasurer of the Western League of minor league baseball. Both stood to lose from Cardinals broadcasts. That brought an end to the threat from Johnson.

Ownership of the Cardinals also helped to ease the threat from the brewery's competition. Anheuser-Busch hired Harry Caray, who had long hyped Griesedieck Brothers beer on Cardinals broadcasts, to sell Budweiser on broadcasts sponsored by the brewery. Griesedieck Brothers, run by part of a German family that had been in the beer business in St. Louis since the 1870s, was first in St. Louis when it had Cardinals broadcasts. After that, A-B had undisputed claim to first place.

Griesedieck Brothers' failure to buy the Redbirds was a factor leading to the 1957 sale of the brand of Falstaff, said Don Roussin, co-author of *St. Louis Brews: 200 Years of Brewing in St. Louis, 1809-2009*. Once again, a conservative company that refused to take a chance lost to an aggressive risk taker. The approach propelled Anheuser-Busch to number one in the country.

People knew Gussie as a sportsman when Anheuser-Busch bought the Cardinals, but only because of his knack as a horseman. He knew nothing about baseball. But he did know marketing. Gussie knew that beer and baseball go together like burgers and fries. Gussie's purchase of the Cardinals changed the way St. Louisans looked at the brewery. Until he died at the end of the 1989 season, Gussie's tutelage over the team in good and bad years helped St. Louisans see him as a jolly old ball club president and not what he was—a hard-nosed corporate exec. The ownership catapulted the brewery to dominance in corporate sponsorship of sports.

A Taste of the
Old Country

ome people came to America for religious freedom. Others came for opportunity or to escape persecution. Helmut Wanninger came from Regensburg, Germany, in the late 1950s because his older brother was going to get the family butcher shop. Big brother Henry Wanninger wound up coming, too, a few years later. With a friend, Otto Gummerscheimer, they founded the firm that today is G&W Bavarian Sausage Co. and started making the same bockwurst, bloodwurst, brockwurst, hausmacher, and bratwurst Helmut and Henry's father and grandfather produced in Bavaria.

Today, Helmut's son Gerhard and Henry's son Bob are still using old family recipes to make their authentic German sausage, plus Cajun-style sausage, Polish sausage, Spanish sausage, Hungarian-style bratwurst, and Italian bratwurst. This festival of nations for sausage is sold at celebrations around town and such places as Grant's Farm, the St. Louis Zoo, Gus's Pretzels, Johnny's Super Market in Sappington, and the Feasting Fox restaurant. G&W's website lists ten kinds of bratwurst, four Landjager or summer sausages, twelve specialty sausages, and five kinds of breads, mustards, and snacks.

The saying goes that lawmaking and sausage-making are two things people shouldn't watch. But Gerhard, who is forty-five, is more than happy to show a visitor how it's done. Behind a showroom with old-style coolers with glass on the front, the work of making the product the old way goes on. The company uses about three thousand to four thousand pounds of pork and beef a week and a few other items to create the stuff for the finest German meals around. Gerhard recalls his father raking hickory sawdust for smoking into an opening below the floor of the family's shop at 4828 Parker Avenue. The smoke would rise into the area where sausage hung. Today, the sawdust goes into a machine where it smolders. A pipe brings the hickory smoke into the room where the sausages are kept. The company also can seal the product in plastic, something that it didn't do years ago. But while the technology is better, the product is the same as it has always been.

Gerhard and Bob are familiar with what real German sausage is like. When their grandparents were still living, they visited the Old Country regularly. They also know that, as a small local operation, they are an anomaly. "There's not too many places like us around," Gerhard said. But as long as people hunger for the taste of a real German brat, the kind that only a little guy can make, there always will be a place for G&W Bavarian Style Sausage.

The Scribbler
with the Bow Tie

reg Marecek was a newly hired kid sports reporter for the *St. Louis Suburban Journals* when an elder statesman invited him to sit at his table at a reception. The older gentleman was the great Bob Broeg, a sports reporter, columnist, and editor of the *St. Louis Post-Dispatch* at a time when presidents read the paper with their morning coffee. Broeg already had developed a legend as the scribe who perpetuated the nickname "The Man" for Stan Musial. Broeg never forgot one of his first reporting jobs scribbling columns for a dime an inch for the *Neighborhood News*, a giveaway paper on the South Side. So it was no surprise back in 1971 that Broeg considered the twenty-two-year-old Marecek an equal and not someone to ignore at a party.

Census documents recorded in St. Louis testify that Broeg was half-German with a sprinkle of English and Irish on the other side. His great-grandfather Heinrich Broeg was Hessian while his great-grandmother came from Prussia. Broeg's grandfather Robert H. was born in Missouri and married another full-blooded German, Julia. Their son, another Robert, broke the pure German line when he married Alice Wiley, who was half Irish and half English. From that union came yet another Robert—Bob, actually—one afternoon in 1918 on the kitchen table of the family's second-floor apartment at Virginia and Pulaski on the South Side. The doctor scratched the infant's left eye with the tongs and blurred Bob's vision for life. Another tong went into the back of his cranium. "So, yeah, I had a hole in my head from day one," he wrote. He remarked that his name in German would have been pronounced "Broog." He laughed when he added that it was "Broeg as in plague."

Young Bob took an interest in sports early on. When the Cardinals won the 1926 World Series, "Neighborhood whistles blew, horns tooted, fireworks exploded and Model-T cars careened," he wrote in his autobiography, *Bob Broeg: Memories of a Hall of Fame Sportswriter.* When an uncle took Bob to his first game at Sportsman's Park on Memorial Day 1927, he was hooked for life. He held on to that love through his years at Cleveland High School and the University of Missouri, where he graduated after Christmas 1940. He always had some kind of sports reporting job and worked for the Associated Press and the old *St. Louis Star-Times* before spending much of World War II in a Marine desk job because of his eyesight. When the war was nearly over, he got his dream assignment as a sports reporter for the *Post-Dispatch.* Life got better in 1946, when his editors switched his beat from the St. Louis Browns to the Redbirds.

Soon Broeg was rubbing elbows with the likes of Joe Garagiola and Red Schoendienst and giving Stanley Frank Musial the moniker people always knew him by. He started using the title "Stan the Man" in 1946, after Cardinals traveling secretary Leo Ward told him Brooklyn Dodgers fans always said, "Here comes the man" when it was Musial's turn to bat. Drinking beer with Browns owner Bill Veeck one Saturday night in August 1951, Broeg got the tip that something very small was about to happen the next day at Sportsman's Park. Broeg alerted *Post-Dispatch* photographer Jack January to keep his camera pointed toward home plate until a new player, the 3-foot 7-inch Eddie Gaedel, came to bat. As Tigers pitcher Bob Cain threw four hopelessly high balls to walk Gaedel, January got the famous pictures of the stunt that most typified Veeck's colorful career. Broeg kept covering stories and gathering memories until he finally gave his pen a rest after his last byline appeared June 20, 2004. The man with the ever-present bow tie officially retired in 1985 but never really stopped. He cranked out at least twenty books before he died on October 28, 2005.

Before he died, Broeg tapped the great baseball writer Rich Hummel as one of the two people to give his eulogy. The other was Marecek, whom Broeg had befriended more than three decades earlier. Broeg stayed close to Marecek as he rose to be a local sports author and broadcaster. "He treated me like a son," said Marecek, founder of the St. Louis Sports Hall of Fame. "He was such a fountain of sports knowledge in St. Louis history. I know right now that Bob is writing a story because he's the sports editor of the *Heavenly Post*."

Bob Broeg and Whitey Herzog

Beer, Bands, and Bunds

or good food and good brew, there was no better place than the Black Forest. When the weather turned sultry, the outer garden of the restaurant at 6432 Gravois Avenue was the place to be. "Waitresses would scurry about, bringing schooners of sudsy beer to thirsty customers at long tables, while the costumed band struck up lively tunes," the *St. Louis Post-Dispatch* said. "A customer who bought the band beer was rewarded by the leader's urging, 'Give him a big hand and make him feel like home.'"

On the eve of the Second World War, however, people worried that more was in the air than polkas and *Gemütlichkeit*. Restaurant owner Peter Heimig grew weary of it all. Friends said he tired of the talk that he was a Nazi sympathizer. So in 1939, he sold the place and bid *auf wiedersehen* to America. He moved his family back home to his native Germany. The *St. Louis Post-Dispatch* said after World War II that Heimig was a local leader of the pro-Nazi *Amerikadeutscher Volksbund* (German-American Bund or German-American political association), which met at the restaurant.

When new managers took over the cafe, Uncle Sam didn't have to worry about treasonous goings-on there, only about getting his fair share. In 1957, the place was closed for non-payment of $7,200 in federal withholding and cabaret taxes. To pay the debt, the IRS sold off furniture and equipment from the bar, kitchen, and dining room. But if the Black Forest Restaurant and Garden is gone, a German element remains at the address. It's now home to the Concordia Turners Gymnastic Society, one of numerous groups Germans founded in the St. Louis area to exercise the mind and body. Also, another restaurant with a similar name, Eisele's Black Forest at 3126 Cherokee Street, made every meal a *fest* until the day it closed in the 1990s. Now as then, the spirit of *Gemütlichkeit* survives at 6432 Gravois Avenue in the Concordia Turners.

Flavorful Food
to Remember

he hasenpfeffer, spaetzel, and sauerbraten at Eisele's Black Forest were enough to make it a favorite for Lester Joern. A dentist who practices not far from Ted Drewes on the South Side, Joern had made the German restaurant at 3126 Cherokee Street a stop for suppers worth remembering. But in the 1980s, Joern had a new reason to remember the place: a waitress named Helga. He had studied German in college but didn't remember much. As he researched his German heritage, he found he needed to read letters sent to him from Germany. Enter Helga. "She used to help me with my German," Dr. Joern said. "She made me order everything in German."

Eisele's Black Forest is one of a long list of elegant German restaurants that closed long ago in St. Louis. So did its sister restaurant, the Bavarian Inn at 3016 Arsenal Street, the German Inn at 4135 South Grand Boulevard, the Golden Horn Restaurant at 6983 Gravois Avenue, the Alpine Inn at 3553 Delor Street, and numerous others. Something about those places made them perfect for making memories.

Ed Golterman, who waged a lonely fight for years to reopen the Kiel Opera House, remembers growing close to his grandfather at German restaurants. Guy Golterman, a key person in the building of what became the Kiel, took him in a Yellow Cab to German restaurants such as Schobers Wine Restaurant at 6925 South Lindbergh Boulevard and the Bismarck Café downtown at 410 North Twelfth Street. Reporters at the Bismarck said hello. Wherever they were, Guy Golterman dropped a little sherry or brandy in his grandson's turtle soup.

Malcolm Magee didn't have as pleasant an experience at the Bavarian Inn at 3016 Arsenal Street in November 1982, but he did make a memory he will never forget. Magee, a professor of history and religion at Michigan State University, lived in St. Louis at the time and sold bearings and power transmission equipment. One day, intent on making a sale, he took a couple of Anheuser-Busch decision makers to the Bavarian Inn. When one ordered "steak tartar," Magee ordered the same.

Then the meal came: "a bloody fresh ground blob of hamburger with a slab of onion topped with a raw egg," he wrote. "Both of them were grinning and I forced myself to continue talking about how our bearings and service were 'the best.'" He was holding it down until he saw blood on the bread. "I grabbed a swig of my iced tea. As I swallowed I noticed that the tallow from the raw meat was coating the inside of my mouth and caused the tea to bead up." Finally, he sent the meat back to be cooked. He didn't make the sale, but he learned a lesson. "From then on I ordered food that had ingredients which had made the acquaintance with the inside of an oven."

St. Louis's Past German Restaurants

Deutschmeister Brass Band

Reconnecting

Berlin's Man in St. Louis

Lansing G. Hecker remembers what it was like to have free time. He remembers hunting and fishing. Hecker, sixty-two, gave that up when he became an agent of a foreign government. Make no mistake. He's a true-blue patriotic American. Nonetheless, being a foreign agent has cost him. He receives nothing for the job. In fact, he must pay his own expenses, which can run three thousand to five thousand dollars a year. But he loves it, in part, because it reminds him of his own heritage.

Since 2004, Hecker has been the honorary consul in Missouri and Southern Illinois for the Federal Republic of Germany. Hecker, who makes his living running a marketing, e-commerce, and sales promotion company, operates below the German consul general in Chicago. "We're a convenience. We're kind of like the local office," he said.

The local office can get busy. At any time, three and a half million German citizens are in the United States, including students, business people, those working in the United States, and tourists. Some visit his home on Saturday morning, when he has office hours. Hecker helps people ship dogs and cats to Germany and can help arrange to send remains of Germans who died in America back home. He notes that if Germans weren't able to perform those tasks at his home, they would have to travel to the office of the consul general in Chicago.

Germans visiting Hecker's house may notice a painting in his living room that hints at why he works so hard. It shows his great-great-grandfather, Friedrich Hecker. A leader of the German uprisings of 1848, he came to America and bought a farm in Summerfield, Illinois, thirty miles east of St. Louis. When the Civil War started, he put together a regiment of German-Americans. It was stuff to make a person proud. But Lansing Hecker didn't realize the importance of his great-great-grandfather until he visited an ancestral home in Germany in 1998.

Soon Lansing Hecker plunged into his heritage, which led him to an active role in the area's German-American community and to his appointment as the area's honorary German consul. His wife, Joan, "participates sometimes and other times lets me do my thing," he said.

Today, he leads the area's German-American Heritage Society and is involved with about twenty-six groups celebrating the local German-American connection. He estimates he attends about a dozen Maifests and eight to ten Oktoberfests each year. He's proud to hold the position because he gets to help people in need far from home. "I get calls at three o'clock in the morning," he said. Often, the caller will say, "My daughter or son won't come home for Christmas." Besides that, he believes his work helps others to be as proud of their German-American heritage as he is of his. Friedrich Hecker would be proud.

Lansing Hecker

St. Louis's honorary consul to Germany

An Oompah Band Brings the Smiles

eter Krege's father learned the fine art of making violins in Berlin before he immigrated to the United States in 1954. So it was inevitable that music would be a part of Peter's life. "I played in a German band in Cleveland," Krege said. "I like the music. I grew up with music in the home." Now Krege, an accountant for the Lutheran Church Missouri Synod, was preparing for a Wednesday night practice of the Deutschmeister Brass Band at the German Cultural Society's Hall at 3652 South Jefferson Avenue. He has played baritone horn for the dozen years he has been with the oompah band.

Although it was just April, the band in 2012 had already scheduled about sixteen performances, including the German Cultural Society's Maifest at Donau-Park in Jefferson County, Oktoberfests at Donau-Park, St. Charles, Lake St. Louis, and Soulard, and a Weihnachtsfeier at the Cultural Society's Hall. At any of those events, band members might play American favorites like the Pennsylvania Polka and the National Anthem. Otherwise, they'll strike up and play the same tunes that bands throughout Germany perform. Germany is full of these bands. It's common for towns and companies to sponsor them. The music here may be a bit behind what the bands in Munich play, but not that much, said Helmuth Glatt, the band's president. "I think it's fun, good camaraderie with all the other band members," Glatt said. He played trumpet in high school but now plays flugelhorn.

Glatt's father, Peter, was a founding member of the band when it formed in 1963 as a subgroup of the German Cultural Society. "We got together and said, 'Why don't we start a brass band?'" said Peter Glatt, who came to America with his family in 1955 from Austria. He was like most of the early members of the band. They were immigrants who already had learned the ways of the German band in Europe. They wanted to keep their tradition alive. Their style and form emulated the German military band of the nineteenth century. They soon became a popular part of local German gatherings. Peter Glatt is not about to quit: "Once you start, it's hard to get away from it."

Glatt was one of four original members of the Deutschmeister listed in the program for the band's Thirtieth Anniversary Celebration on April 24, 1993. That program contained congratulatory ads from at least two other local German bands, the Wendl Band and the Waterloo German Band. Others buying ads included Eisele's Black Forest and Bavarian Inn and the St. Louis Strassenfest Corporation. The main speaker was the last German mayor of St. Louis, Vincent C. Schoemehl, right after he retired.

Today, Nellie Eddleman directs the band. A former public school band director, she has been a part of the Deutschmeister since the mid-1980s. "These are my guys to yell at. These are my guys to whip into shape," Eddleman said. On Sunday, April 15, 2012, Eddleman was at it, whipping her guys into shape at the Wurstmarkt at the German Cultural Society's Hall. Out at long narrow brown tables, men, woman, and children feasted on sausage, sauerkraut, and beer. On the tile dance floor, a teenage girl in a traditional dirndl danced with a much-younger girl. A gray-haired couple got up to dance. Others joined in. On the stage, red-fringed banners festooned with the words, "Deutschmeister Brass Band St. Louis Mo." adorned music stands in the front row. Band members with tubas, trumpets, and drums wore bright red vests. Eddle-man moved her hands to the rousing sound of polkas, waltzes, and marches. Once, after a tune began, she left her post and returned with a pitcher of beer and cups for thirsty band members. "The tubas are 'oom.' Your trombones and French horns would be the 'pah,'" Eddle-man said during a break, explaining how one repeated sound makes this an "oompah" band. When the band played its last "oompah," everyone had a smile.

Good Food from the Fatherland

hen it comes time to eat, German food is as straight-forward and intense as Germans themselves. Potato pancakes are simple but anything but boring. Beef is soaked for days in red wine and spiced brine to make sauerbraten. Bratwurst is packed with finely ground pork or beef, cooked in beer, and smothered with pungent horseradish, mustard, or sauerkraut. That sauerkraut, by the way, is pickled in brine for weeks to let the *lactobacillus* bacteria do its work. Add a bottle of Paulner, Hofbrau, or Spatan and the meal is complete. It's true that St. Louis doesn't have a lot of restaurants that specialize in German fare. But there are enough to please the palate. A sampling:

When Ann Sueme and her sister Maritza Stock and Maritza's husband, Bill, went to work renovating a broken-down building at 1740 Chouteau Avenue in 2003, things didn't seem hopeful. But before long, what once had been a haven for gangs was reborn as the St. Louis Gast Haus. Today, one wall is a ceiling-to-floor mural of Berlin's Brandenberg Gate, complete with brilliant dark blue sky, a red-orange sunset, and yellow buildings. On white tablecloths, customers of the Gast Haus savor German food.

For those wanting a German restaurant with a sports flair, the place to be is the Rhine Haus Eatery and Pub at 255 Union Boulevard just north of Forest Park. It's a sports bar with a mix of German and pub food. Among its specialties: the Frickadellen, a German burger made of pork and beef, the triple-decker reuben, and the standard fare expected at German eateries.

The Schneithorst restaurant now at Clayton Road and Lindbergh Boulevard doesn't have the elegance of the Schneithorst Hofamberg Inn that once was at the location. The Hofamberg Inn opened in 1956, nearly a half century after the family opened its first restaurant. After it closed in 2002, a new Schneithorst restaurant opened for a more general clientele. But it kept a limited selection of German foods. Patrons at the restaurant can order such foods as German Pizza, a knackwurst reuben, and the Milwaukee Club. A favorite since 1917, the Milwaukee Club includes braunschweiger, bacon, lettuce, tomato, red onion, and mayonnaise on rye bread.

On the South Side, some selections at two restaurants continue the German tradition started at both places by the German-American August A. Busch Sr. when he had Anheuser-Busch build them before Prohibition. The Sunday morning and afternoon buffet at the Bevo Mill, 4749 Gravois Avenue, includes German delights like braised red cabbage, knockwurst, and a potato pancake station among its other fare. And at Al Smith's Feasting Fox Restaurant and Pub at 4200 South Grand Boulevard, owners Martin and Susan Luepker serve such favorites as German black bean soup, Black Forest sweet and sour pork, and Holsteiner schnitzel.

You will find old German family recipes handed down to Joan Lang at Dreamland Palace in Foster Pond in rural Monroe County. Lang and her husband, Mike, welcome customers in a 136-year-old building four miles west of Waterloo on Illinois Route 156. Before the Langs bought the place in 1990, it served variously as a stagecoach stop, general store, dance hall, and tavern. The German foods from Joan's cookbook are sure to make the extra drive worth it.

Roemer Topf, in Mascoutah, also is on the east side of the river. Roemer Topf is a clay cooking vessel popular in Bavaria. So it shouldn't be a surprise that Renate Gray named a restaurant featuring food from her home in Bavaria "Roemer Topf." Gray, who opened the restaurant at 1415 McKinley Road five years ago, works with her brother, Robert Iwan, the chef, and her son, Michael Schoelzel. Bavarian specialties mix with more traditional German fare, but the regional Bavarian emphasis is obvious. Gray explains it this way: "In Boston, you eat different things than in New Orleans, but you're in the same country."

In Belleville, many Friday and Saturday nights are Germanfest at the Shrine Restaurant at the National Shrine of Our Lady of the Snows in Belleville. A buffet at the restaurant at 442 S. DeMazenod Drive features such German fare as spaetzle, bratwurst and sauerkraut, schwein schnitzel, and apple strudel. There's a variety of places to find German food. Hearty is a word to describe it, consumed in good company, with a smile and the spirit of *Gemütlichkeit.*

Guten Appetit!

The Fests of Oktober

small school bus stops at a sidewalk next to Lyon Park and discharges a load of about thirty passengers dressed in lederhosen and dirndls. The air on South Broadway is alive with the sound of sometimes-intelligible music from the park, a short walk from the Anheuser-Busch Brewery. Signs on a chain-link fence around the park indicate what's in store. "Jagermeister," "Budweiser," say two signs, read by revelers in a long line. Another, sponsored by Budweiser and Laclede Cab, encourages everyone to call a cab rather than drive drunk. "*Wilkommen Zum* Soulard Oktoberfest," states a final sign, near where workers take five-dollar admission fees.

Kyle Osterhage, who just stepped off the bus, was ready with his dark green hat and his short dark green pants. "I get in free with the getup," said Osterhage, an insurance sales rep who was part of a group celebrating his brother's birthday at the Soulard Oktoberfest. "It's just showing our heritage." He loves the dress and the German beer. It's impossible to avoid that beer, ever-present beneath the white circus tents and out in the open and next to stages where the likes of Brave Combo, Polka Floyd, and Dorfrocker soon would perform. "You drink a lot of beer, and you eat a lot of food," said Nick Baur, a trumpet player in St. Louis's Deutschmeister Brass Band, which entertained at the Soulard Oktoberfest.

The Soulard Oktoberfest has appeared on at least one American Oktoberfest top ten list. Cincinnati's, however, is the largest in the country and the second largest in the world. Cincinnati brags that the more than half-million who show up each year consume 80,500 brats and 3,600 pounds of sauerkraut, not to mention beer. That's nothing compared to the Oktoberfest in Munich, Germany. The seventeen-day festival began in 1810 to honor the marriage of Bavarian Crown Prince

Ludwig to Princess Therese von Sachsen-Hildburghausen. From this celebration came all the German parties of fall.

"The whole thing's built around beer," said Edward Hecker, great-great-grandson of German revolutionary and Civil War fighter Friedrich Hecker, who settled on a farm twenty-eight miles east of St. Louis. Edward, a St. Louisan, has attended the local Oktoberfest as well as Munich's. In daytime, the Munich Oktoberfest is for families, he claimed. At night, it's like a frat party. It's huge, overwhelming anything in St. Louis.

But bigger needn't mean more fun, whether in Soulard or elsewhere in the St. Louis area. In St. Charles, a main feature of the Oktoberfest is the Wiener Takes All races. Dachshunds square off in such categories as Little Smokies (sixteen weeks to one year old), Five Footers (one to five years old), and aged sausages (five and older). In Jefferson County, the German Cultural Society holds a small and warm celebration at its Donau-Park centered on dancing, music, cuisine, and activities for kids.

Oktoberfest in the hamlet of Maeystown, Illinois—southwest of Waterloo—means arts, crafts, and an antique fair. In Belleville, the 2011 celebration featured the oldies band Sh-Boom, magicians, pumpkin decorating, and clowns. Local bars often hold Oktoberfests as a way to sell more beer in October. If he were still around, Crown Prince Ludwig might decide how much each of these fetes live up to what he had in mind for his wedding celebration. Since he's not here, it's up to the individual to settle the matter of authenticity—over brats and Franziskaner, of course.

. . . Und Mai

art, really tart, potato salad, on a foam plate next to cole slaw swimming in vinegar helped to put one and all in the mood for Maifest. Two well-done fully juiced brats topped with bread on the same plate made the preparation complete. The holder of that plate eyed the brats, hungrily looking forward to the moment when he would bite down on the prize. The visitor had the option of golden brown fried chicken. Some chose it, but at the risk of losing the mood of a Bavarian village. A hot Bavarian village, to be sure, because the German Cultural Society's Donau-Park in Jefferson County still is in the St. Louis area, and it was May 20. Almost summer.

No matter. Good beer added to the German tone, as did the sight of men young and old in shorts, white shirts, and distinctive suspenders. Women and girls of all ages were in the traditional dress of Germany as well. Blue seemed to be a popular color for women's German outfits, as diners sought rare space on tables in a main pavilion. The Deutsch-meister Brass Band provided the oompah music, but only for a while. A group of young dancers in traditional outfits took over and danced around the Mai Pole. One of the dancers wore a button: "Kiss me. I'm German."

Gerard Schellin, wearing lederhosen, was selling handcrafted German wooden toys: cuckoo clocks, Black Forest weathervanes, mushrooms, a man playing a bass fiddle, and a cook with a blue plaid apron. The most distinctive quality about lederhosen is the horizontal connection between the two suspenders in the front. Often, it is decorated with a design. The shorts also can have a design on them. A felt hat adds to the look. Schellin's bushy mustache added to the Germanic look. He sells the craft items at German Cultural Society events. "It means a lot to me. It's part of my heritage," Schellin said. His parents arrived in America separately in 1951, met, and married. His mother, Ruth, came from Silesia, Poland. His father, Hermann, came from an area that once was part of East Germany and now is in Poland. Ruth has been attending Maifest for years. She loves the food and the music. "We used to dance to it, but I can't do that any more," she said.

This was Ernest Morfeld's first Maifest. His German ancestors settled in Osage County, Missouri, in 1840. His great-great-grandfather was a corporal in the Union Calvary, part of a group that protected Jefferson City. On Easter, he follows the German tradition of having an Easter tree. "It's pride in finding where I came from," said Morfeld.

Maifest is fun, but Bruno Erben isn't sure how long it can last. Erben, who came from the north-central part of Germany, worries that the old German immigrants are dying out and won't be replaced. "Most of the German societies are gone," said Erben, who once was president of a German singing society. He believes that the German language is dying out in the region. In ten or twenty years, there won't be much left, he predicted. Meanwhile, in the pavilion, young dancers kept up their dance.

Speaking German on Saturday Mornings

t's Saturday morning, and five-year-old Ava Martin should be at home watching cartoons or playing video games. Instead, she is in school, learning that a hat is a *hut*, a dress is a *kleiden*, and an elbow is an *ellbogen*. Meanwhile, her father, thirty-nine-year-old Jim Martin, is down the hallway learning advanced German conversation. Both are among about 170 adults and children who attend classes of the German School Association of Greater St. Louis on Saturday mornings from September to May at St. Paul's Lutheran Church in Des Peres. Many of the students see the class as a way to reconnect with their past. "My family came from Germany in the late 1800s," said Martin. "My grandmother spoke German in the home. My parents didn't know any German." He studied German in college and in his five months at the University of Heidelberg in Germany. Now he is the vice president of the German School Association's board of directors.

"They see this as a way to keep their heritage alive," said Helga Thalheimer, president of the board of directors. She has been a teacher at the school since 1993, and she was present when the school had its first classes in the 1960s. Her mother was an ethnic German from Romania, and her father an ethnic German from Yugoslavia. "I had to learn English when I started kindergarten," Thalheimer said. Her father, Jakob, founded the school in 1962 along with Andrew Roeslein and Conrad Geislinger. Helga Thalheimer never had formal training in teaching, but it's clear from her first-year German class for eight-to-twelve-year-olds that she knows how to keep her pupils involved. She writes German words on a white board, then walks up and down the aisle speaking to children as she goes.

When the school started, many of the students were the children of immigrants. Now, they are in the second and third generations. About 20 to 30 percent of students are from the German community. The rest are children and adults who want to learn German. A good number of the children are home schooled. "We get a lot of people who want to do their genealogy," Thalheimer said. The school charges $350 a year for thirty three-hour sessions taught by paid German teachers or native German speakers.

Gabriele Steinhauff, who came from Frankfurt, Germany, as a child, teaches adults. "We have a highly diverse class of professionals that love to learn the German language," she said. Jim Morrison and Gary McKiddy are in Steinhauff's advanced conversation class with Martin. Morrison is an insurance underwriter who was born in Switzerland to missionaries who were stationed near Zurich. He spent the first six or seven years of his life speaking German there and still has a bit of an accent. "I really do enjoy the German language. It keeps that connection to my original birthplace," said Morrison.

Gary McKiddy, a teacher at St. Charles Community College, was born with a mix of Irish, Scottish, and German blood. His wife, Gale, teaches for the German School Association and studied abroad in her junior year in college at the Teachers University in Dortmund, Germany. McKiddy has been studying at the school for six or seven years and is on its board of directors. "My wife got me involved, and I did German as my research language for my doctorate," but he still wasn't very good. "We'd go to Germany, and I'd sit there and be stupid." With the German language training he and others receive from the German School Association, McKiddy sounds anything but stupid when he speaks German.

Peace Through Understanding

hen the Mississippi River at St. Louis reached record levels in the Flood of 1993, the city received help from an unexpected source. Citizens of the German city of Stuttgart reached into their wallets and contributed $11,000 for local flood relief, to be divided between the Salvation Army and the American Red Cross. They did it as part of a bond of friendship forged in 1960 when representatives from St. Louis and Stuttgart signed papers uniting the two communities as sister cities. Their agreement was part of an effort by then-President Dwight D. Eisenhower to foster peace by understanding others better. Since then, St. Louis–Stuttgart Sister Cities, Inc. has promoted exchanges of students and business people, efforts to showcase the musical and artistic talents, and numerous other projects to increase understanding of both cities' cultures.

Smaller towns surrounding St. Louis have made similar pacts with comparable towns in Germany and around the world. In Columbia, Illinois, large numbers of citizens and students frequently fly to their sister city of Gedern, Germany. People from Gedern frequently reciprocate and come to Columbia. The visits are a major part of life in both communities, complete with handshakes of old friends and pictures in the local papers. Although the two towns approved a declaration of friendship in 1992, links actually began 150 years before that. In 1842, 118 adults and 38 children emigrated from Wernings, Germany (now Gedern), and settled in the area of Columbia and Waterloo, Illinois.

Waterloo has its own sister city relationship with Porta Westfalica, Germany. Each June, it toasts that bond in its Porta Westfalica Fest. Visitors from Germany are often among those reveling around the courthouse square. In Belleville, Illinois, civic leaders sealed their sister cities agreement in 1990 with Paderborn, North Rhine-Westfalia,

Germany. Marbach am Neckar, Germany, the birthplace of German poet, dramatist, and philosopher Johann Christoph Friedrich von Schiller, is the sister city of Washington, Missouri, a town with a strong German heritage. And St. Charles, Missouri, has celebrated its bond with its German sister city of Ludwigsburg with student exchanges, a Deutschfest Dinner Dance, church services, and a visit from the mayor of Ludwigsburg.

St. Louis's relationship with Stuttgart, meanwhile, is hardly limited to St. Louis's city limits. People join from Kirkwood, Chesterfield, and places in between. Members of the St. Louis–Stuttgart Sister Cities group have found housing for members of large bands and delegations from universities. "The Germans always love to go to Hannibal. They love Mark Twain," said Roy Leimberg, a St. Louis Hills resident who has been involved in the St. Louis–Stuttgart Sister Cities group since 1986. Christi Roeder, of Webster Groves, who is majoring in secondary education and German and minoring in Japanese at the University of Missouri, is among the students the group has helped get to Stuttgart. The organization partially funded her trip to a UNESCO World Youth Conference in Stuttgart in 2008 and another trip to Stuttgart in 2010 to celebrate the fiftieth anniversary of the St. Louis–Stuttgart Sister Cities union. She went with her bluegrass band. "(It) helped me to really fuel my interest in German language and German culture," Roeder said. The St. Louis–Stuttgart group also partially funds the exchange trips of high school exchange students to Stuttgart and welcomes exchange students coming to St. Louis from Stuttgart. The trips to Stuttgart have a sharp effect on students from St. Louis, said Michael King, a pharmacist who is in charge of the organization's youth program. When they return, "They usually have a new outlook on life," he said.